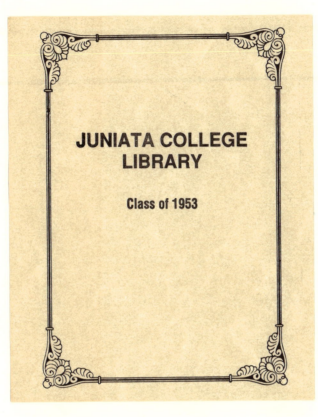

Mark Twain
and
William James

Mark Twain
and
William James

Crafting a Free Self

Jason Gary Horn

University of Missouri Press
Columbia and London

Library of Congress Cataloging-in-Publication Data

Horn, Jason Gary, 1951–
      Mark Twain and William James : crafting a free self / Jason
      Gary Horn.
          p. cm.
      Includes bibliographical references and index.
      ISBN 0-8262-1072-4 (alk. paper)
      1. Twain, Mark, 1835–1910—Knowledge—Psychology. 2. Twain,
Mark, 1835–1910. Personal recollections of Joan of Arc. 3. Twain,
Mark, 1835–1910. Adventures of Huckleberry Finn. 4. Twain, Mark,
1835–1910. Mysterious stranger. 5. James, William, 1842–1910—
Influence. 6. Consciousness in literature. 7. Psychology in literature.
8. Self in literature.   I. Title.
PS1342.P74H67   1996
818'.409—dc20   96-25515
                                                                                        CIP

∞™ This paper meets the requirements of the
American National Standard for Permanence of Paper
for Printed Library Materials, Z39.48, 1984.

Designer: Stephanie Foley
Printer and binder: Thomson-Shore, Inc.
Typeface: Garamond

For Edward Peter Nolan

mentor, friend, and kind soul

I have already insisted on the fact that truth is made largely out of previous truths. Men's beliefs at any time are so much experience *funded*. But the beliefs are themselves parts of the sum total of the world's experience, and become matter, therefore, for the next day's funding operations. . . . But these beliefs make us act, and as fast as they do, they bring into sight or into existence new facts which re-determine the beliefs accordingly. So the whole coil and ball of truth, as it rolls up, is the product of a double influence. Truths emerge from facts; but they dip forward into facts again and add to them; which facts again create or reveal new truth (the word is indifferent) and so on indefinitely. The "facts" themselves meanwhile are not *true*. They simply *are*. Truth is the function of the beliefs that start and terminate among them.

William James, *Pragmatism*

—— CONTENTS ——

ACKNOWLEDGMENTS

Let me first of all recognize the late Edward Peter Nolan, without whom this book would still be little more than hopes and dreams. From the earliest drafts of often ill-conceived chapters, Nolan was available as a teacher and guide; he soon became a friend as well. He believed in me and my project, and without his wisdom and knowledge this book would have come to an early end. His critical acumen helped to provide it with whatever cogent and significant ideas it may contain. Nolan was still teaching at the University of Colorado at Boulder when he died on October 26, 1994. Nolan was devoted to his own work in medieval studies and comparative literature; he was diligently involved in the work of those under his tutelage; he was a passionate participant in the shaping of knowledge.

Along with Nolan, others at the University of Colorado at Boulder were amenable to my project as well. My conversations with John Murphy about American pragmatism and its seminal figures provided a continual and delightful source of intellectual stimulation; his uncanny ability to traverse and integrate wide ranges of thought was always inspiring. Bruce Kawin, Nan Goodman, Fred Denny, and Margaret Ferguson read an early version of the manuscript and offered fruitful advice on its weaknesses. Ferguson, in particular, was kind enough to read and reread each chapter, surely a demanding chore, and she offered precise and detailed observations on style and clarity—or lack thereof.

Still others must be acknowledged for helping me complete the book. Without the encouragement of Carroll Peterson, I would have abandoned my studies many years ago. His commitment to teaching and love of literature have been a continual inspiration.

In a timely manner, Emily C. Walhout of the Houghton Library located and allowed me to view letters that Twain and James had exchanged, and Victor Fisher and Brenda Bailey of the Mark Twain Project sent necessary copies of new and unpublished material from Twain's manuscripts and notebooks. I owe a special debt to Judge Harry Pregerson, who owns Twain's copy of James's *Varieties of Religious Experience*. He was more than willing to help in my research and kindly permitted me to view and quote from Twain's previously unpublished marginalia.

At the University of Northern Colorado, the staff members at the James Michener Library were more than gracious with their time and support. The reference librarians directed me toward useful and pertinent texts, sometimes seemingly lost documents, and the staff in periodicals granted me extended use of necessary material. Through the efforts of the interlibrary loan department, especially those of Lois Leffler, I was able to track down and borrow rare and out-of-print books, little-known essays, and special microfilm material.

The staff, faculty, and friends in the English department at the University of Northern Colorado were equally supportive. The department's familial atmosphere helped to create a pleasant working environment, one that still exists to a large degree because of the sincere concern shown by Pat Chandler and Lyndalee Berger for the people involved in the department's daily operations. Among the English faculty, I should like to thank Rita Kiefer and Lloyd Worley for their spiritually satisfying conversations, Ben Varner for his pragmatic advice, Tomas Santos for listening to my worries about the manuscript, Sharon Riesberg, John Brand, and Edward Kearns for sharing their views on Twain, John Harrison for his always insightful discussions, and Joonuk Huh, Sharon Wilson, Phyllis Endicott, and Becky Edgerton for their warm support and encouragement. John Loftis and Elizabeth Jane Wall Hinds read and commented on my introductory chapter and lifted my spirits at a time when my enthusiasm was flagging. Hinds also introduced me to Norman Grabo, whose suggestions have enabled me to see my subject in the larger context of American religious thought. Indeed I wish to express my gratitude to all my colleagues for enduring what must have seemed like an excessive amount of chatter about the thoughts and writings of Twain and James.

A few close friends need to be mentioned here as well, since they suffered through much of the same incessant talk. Through many provocative conversations, Joseph and Deirdre MacLaren helped me to clarify my intentions and solidify my ideas. Their passion for life and literature more than once enkindled my own and revitalized my thinking and convictions. In much the same way, my conversations with Peter Williams and Bradley Arnold, while we were graduate students at the University of Colorado at Boulder, were forever stimulating. Williams and Arnold challenged me to sift through many of my beliefs and reconsider the consequences of acting upon them.

To my wife, Sharon, I owe more than I can say for enduring my preoccupation with this book. I have been constantly reading, writing, and talking about Twain and James for the past five years, and she has raised few objections. More than this, she has patiently reminded me of the importance of life outside the pale of books and literary study.

A section of chapter 2 was originally published in *Studies in American Fiction*. It is reprinted by permission of its editor Mary Loeffelholz and Northeastern University. A much briefer version of chapter 3 appeared in *Arizona Quarterly, A Journal of American Literature, Culture, and Theory,* copyright 1996 by the Arizona Board of Regents. It is reprinted by permission of its editor Edgar A. Dryden and the University of Arizona. A portion of chapter 3 was presented as a paper at the 1994 conference of the Rocky Mountain Modern Language Association in Colorado Springs, Colorado. Finally, my gratitude goes out to the editors at the University of Missouri Press for their time spent in reading and delivering this book in a presentable form.

Mark Twain
and
William James

Sounding Mark Twain against William James

It was pretty ornery preaching . . . but everybody said it was a good sermon . . . and had such a powerful lot to say about faith, and good works, and free grace, and preforeordestination, and I don't know what all, that it did seem to me to be one of the roughest Sundays I had run across yet.

> —Mark Twain, *Adventures of Huckleberry Finn*

T his book offers a significant revision of one of America's important, endearing, and yet intellectually undersung writers, Mark Twain. A fresh look at his later years shows that far from shrinking into a kind of literary senility, as too many critics have implied, Twain actually grew in imaginative strength during the last two decades of his life. He continued to develop his art and intellect as his century closed and the next one opened. Even as the deaths of family and friends closed his intimate relations with them—most painfully with his wife, Olivia—Twain refused to resign himself to the shadow of mortality. Instead his intellect flourished outside the pale of circumstance. Much of his late work, in fact, reveals an attempt to artistically render, or figure forth, the very nature of intellect itself, the potential power of mind to shape and create its world. Thinking the world into shape, however, means believing in the free agency of mind, a freedom of thought that ultimately equates the human with the divine. Struggling against his sense of cosmic determinism and all too aware of human limitations, Twain nonetheless celebrated such godlike thinking in his work by evoking the experience of freedom through images of divided selves.

This book focuses, then, upon the experience of freedom and what I am calling Mark Twain's religious psychology of the divided self. More precisely, the following chapters work to reconstruct the implied possibilities of independent thought and action within that psychology embodied in three texts of Twain's: *Adventures of Huckleberry Finn, Personal Recollections of Joan of Arc,* and *No. 44, The Mysterious Stranger.* These texts encapsulate both Twain's early and late theoretical speculations on the nature of a divided self. From the thoughts and actions of the protagonists figured in these works, we can trace and follow Twain's fictive map of mind, which eventually leads to a new vision of personal freedom.

Twain, of course, was hardly alone in his speculations upon the problems of "duality," a nineteenth-century term for what we may call the experience of the "self" in the face of the "other." Philosophy has long pondered the central seductions and dangers of dualism. Emerson was the major force in nineteenth-century American philosophy, and the famous "transparent eye-ball" image in his early essay "Nature" reveals Emerson's desire both to resolve the dilemma and to define, if not actually dissolve, the self within a divine other. Indeed, the diffusive experience, as Emerson perceived it, revealing nature's "dear and connate" relationship, momentarily suspends otherness in a commingling that, at least for Emerson, frees the self within the unlimited parameters of that other. Emerson resolved the problem of duality, then, by implicitly denying its essential reality while projecting the apparent experience of it into a potentially divine selfhood.[1]

Twain's own developing concerns with this ontological and epistemological paradox point to a similar desire to evoke and articulate the self's dual energies, yet his explorations of consciousness in the characters of Huck Finn, Joan of Arc, and August Feldner, whom I have chosen as interpretive targets, reveal only tentative, ambivalent acceptance of Emerson's undying faith in human godhood. Believing Twain less ambivalent, James Johnson specifically frames the cumulative imagery of Twain's literary characters in the transcendental language of Emerson. In his *Mark Twain and the Limits of Power: Emerson's God in Ruins,* Johnson locates Twain within Emerson's

---

1. Ralph Waldo Emerson, "Nature," 6.

attempt to realize an ideal selfhood upon the world. However, he sees Twain's efforts to do so as futile and self-destructive, leading eventually to a solipsistic denial of all experience outside the domain of the ego. In the end, though, Twain refuses to let his characters completely fade away into a comforting seclusion of mind or, for that matter, the blissful transparency of certainty. They enact their presence in and upon the world within the psychomachia of the self realized through interior dialogue.

Although Twain certainly knew Emerson's work, praising it at times while burlesquing it at others, his literary responses were fostered in a different social and intellectual climate. Twain's idealism could not be as optimistically surefooted as Emerson's antebellum certainty. Moreover, by the latter quarter of the century—when the world was coming to terms with the full implications of Darwinian theory—Emerson's transcendental faith in human divinity was difficult to maintain on its own terms. It was not because the faith, itself, floundered; instead, within the skeptical horizons of late-nineteenth-century America, its appropriation required an interceding vocabulary and a new perspective. When we turn toward William James, we find what we are looking for: one who not only articulated the hopes and doubts of a generation but also cast an influential shadow as wide as Emerson's own.

James will provide us with the necessary plumb line for sounding the voice of Mark Twain, for ascertaining the depth of his intellect. Like Emerson, James was a cultural bellwether. He taught within the confines of Harvard, but he also directed much of his efforts toward the general public, often delivering popular lectures and writing for popular journals. Both literary and philosophical camps embraced him as one of their own, as did an eclectic group of the social, political, and religious theorists of his day. His work in psychology, of course, influenced not only his colleagues but also generations to follow within and across several disciplinary boundaries. James's correspondence alone reveals a wide array of interests and a "peculiar genius," as Ralph Barton Perry calls it, for entering into "relations of intimacy" with a large and diverse circle of contemporaries.[2] And

2. Ralph Barton Perry, *The Thought and Character of William James*, 1:ix. This work is indispensable. Perry provides not only a detailed account of James's life but also the historical and intellectual background necessary for understanding James's evolving interests.

although the humorist from Hannibal may seem to many an unlikely companion for the professor from Harvard, the fact is that Mark Twain and William James entered into and nurtured a friendship, interweaving their often complementary strands of thought.

The first documented meeting between Twain and James took place while both vacationed with their families in Florence, Italy, in 1892. "I have seen him a couple of times," James wrote home to Josiah Royce, "a fine, soft, fibred little fellow with the perversest twang and drawl, but very human and good. One might grow very fond of him," he confessed, "and wish he'd come and live in Cambridge." And a month later, in a letter to Francis Boott, James lightheartedly wrote about dining with Twain and his disappointment in having "no chance afterwards to ask him to sing Nora McCarty." "He's a dear man," though, "and there'll be a chance yet."[3]

Both Twain and James, when not indulging their appetite for food, song, and conversation, found time for work. In fact, each was enjoying a burst of inspiration. Following his remarks about Twain in his letter to Royce, James wrote about a general reawakening in "matters philosophical," arousing ideas for a new work following his bout with a "sort of mental palsy" over the last year. Twain, too, as James explained in his letter to Francis Boott, "says he has written more in the past four months than he could have done in two years at Hartford."[4] James's letter points to the particular surge of energy that carried Twain through more than half of his *Personal Recollections of Joan of Arc* before his leaving Florence. And Twain's remarks to James reveal an accurate knowledge of his own working habits and the social pressures of Hartford. *Joan of Arc* was not finished until 1895.

The fraternizing at Florence left Twain with more than just warm memories. He came away with a copy of *The Principles of Psychology*. The notes he made in Florence point to the purchase of James's seminal work, though Twain may have instead acquired the shorter *Psychology: The Briefer Course* published in 1892. Written evidence that Twain read the book comes from his own notations and acknowledgments, which he made a few years after his initial pur-

3. William James, *The Letters of William James,* 1:333, 341–42.
4. Ibid.

chase. In his 1896 notebook, he entered a direct quotation from James's "Habit."[5] James's chapter centers upon a topic Twain more commonly referred to as "training," his term for the host of cultural and environmental influences that condition thought and action. The subject of training and the extent of its determining influence, as well as the extent to which one might act freely within its parameters, had haunted Twain's imagination at least since the writing of his *Adventures of Huckleberry Finn.* In the central drama of that text, as Huck wavers between committing himself to hell or Jim, Twain posits the reality of a divided self against even his own deterministic leanings, which necessitated a notion of duality that allows for autonomous action apart from conditioning forces.

Although Twain would never particularly use the term *divided self,* his presentation of Huck's struggle with conscience anticipates his later speculations on the self's dual energies and reflects his earlier attempts to depict the double nature of identity. In a lengthy passage originally a part of "My Platonic Sweetheart," written in 1898 though deleted from the version posthumously published in *Harper's* magazine in 1912, Twain speculated specifically on his own idea of the divided self. In this digression from his story's main concern, a recurring, spiritually satisfying dream affair with an eternally young and innocent sweetheart, Twain connected himself directly with the thought and psychological work of William James.

Thinking back over the years in "My Platonic Sweetheart," Twain recalled his 1876 article "The Facts Concerning the Recent Carnival of Crime in Connecticut." It depicted him struggling with his conscience, which he portrayed as an independent entity bent on freeing itself from its guest host. The article, he explains, was a "crude attempt to work out the duality idea" which "the investigations made by our Professor William James" and certain "French experiments in hypnotism seem to clearly demonstrate." Twain failed to mention the names of the particular French investigators, but did note in his 1898 story

---

5. My information comes from Alan Gribben's *Mark Twain's Library: A Reconstruction,* 1:351. Without Gribben's reconstruction of Twain's library, my own argument for the intertextual and interpersonal relationship shared by Mark Twain and William James would suffer. Gribben's work allowed me to locate Twain more convincingly within the theoretical discourses of James. See James, "Habit," in *The Principles of Psychology,* Vol. 1.

of platonic intimacy that their experiments were made "ten or twelve years ago." Most likely, he was pointing to the work of prominent psychotherapists Jean Charcot and Pierre Janet, both of whom attended, as did William James, the First International Congress of Experimental Psychology held in Paris in 1889. For Twain, such clarifying investigations could only confirm his belief that "two persons" with "quite opposite characters" did indeed inhabit one body.[6]

Twain's earliest attempt to fictionally portray dual personalities suggests, as Minnie M. Brashear points out in her discussion of Twain's reading habits, his reworking of an age-old theme, one that Poe had previously used in his work. Interpreting Twain's claim that he knew nothing about books as an attempt to sell himself as an original American author, Brashear notes his "apparent indebtedness" to Poe's "William Wilson" in particular and suggests that the personification of conscience as it enters Twain's "Carnival of Crime" perched upon a bookcase must surely be a burlesque of Poe's raven.[7] Whether comically resisting Poe's influence or embracing his thought, in his "Carnival of Crime," Twain set forth his ideas on conscience and its divisive attempts to dominate its human host. With his *Adventures of Huckleberry Finn,* however, Twain moved beyond presenting the interior other solely in terms of a tormenting conscience.

While Twain still centered the decisive action of *Huckleberry Finn* around Huck's conscientious struggles, he no longer presented conscience itself as an embodied other. Huck's interior dialogue reveals instead that conscience exists as a product of training, while his actions suggest an encounter with a presence outside the bounds of such a determining influence but still within the expansive margins of the self. For both Twain and James, such an encounter provided a means for constructing a new vision of the human possibility for freedom in the face of an array of rather bleak indicators of the eternal presence of a cosmic determinism. The possibility of acting freely through the self's duality, or within multiple layers of consciousness, points to a later and even more critical acknowledgment of the importance of James's *Psychology* for Twain. Although Twain would

6. My reference is to the unpublished manuscript and typescript of "My Platonic Sweetheart," Mark Twain Papers, Bancroft Library, University of California, Berkeley.

7. Minnie M. Brashear, *Mark Twain: Son of Missouri,* 212–13.

not have studied James's *Psychology* in the same manner as the Harvard professor's own students did, his deference to James's authority on the subject of duality points to more than just a casual reading. In fact, the particular "investigations," which Twain accepted as affirming his own long-standing belief in a divided self, weave their way through James's *Psychology* and find their tentative conclusions primarily in "The Consciousness of Self," a chapter that descriptively argues the case for "double" or "alternate" personalities.[8] His argument eventually finds its way into *No. 44, The Mysterious Stranger,* Twain's boldest attempt to present his own investigations into the divided self and into the potentially creative and ameliorative power drawn from inward division. This approach to inward division locates both men within what we might call a religio-pragmatic perspective on the problem of duality.

Sigmund Freud would later provide the twentieth century with a method of analyzing and "healing" inner division, thus viewing the split as primarily a disabling disease. Meanwhile, R. D. Laing, interpreting Freudian psychology as a species of existential philosophy, described the phenomenon of the divided self less as a sign of disease than as an expression of authentic existence, one that becomes pathological only when the sense of split is excessively exacerbated. It is worth briefly attending to Laing's speculations on the divided self here before turning specifically to those of Twain and James. In many ways, Laing's thinking resembles James's and Twain's; building upon Freud, it may also enhance much of our own present knowledge of ourselves. Laing's perspective, that is to say, is just different enough to provide the useful distinctions necessary for clarifying our inquiry into the thinking of Twain and James.

In his book on inward division, appropriately titled *The Divided Self,* Laing attempted to integrate a phenomenological or existential approach into a more clinical focus on "schizoid" and "schizophrenic" personalities. Like James, Laing believed that all of us are open to experiencing a separation of the self from the body, especially during those overwhelming moments when events seem more like a dream than reality. For Laing, however, the acute schizoid individual experiences a "rent in his relation with his world" and may feel "per-

---

8. William James, *The Principles of Psychology,* 1:379. Subsequent references will be given parenthetically in the text.

secuted by reality itself"; he then seeks to "transcend the world" by "psychical withdrawal," which in turn divides the self between its own secure inner world and the threatening world outside.[9]

Laing further explained that for the ontologically insecure person, whose secure "sense of self" is threatened by "ordinary circumstances," the ultimate effect of such "inner defensive maneuvers" is, paradoxically, the "apparent eventual destruction and dissolution of the self." The schizoid individual, according to Laing, constructs a world of fantasy in which to protect the inner self and to avoid directly experiencing outward social reality. Laing centered his approach upon the detrimental effects of this withdrawal into an illusory world, and thus approached the issue of a divided self, or the "schizoid condition," as leading to a "deterioration and disintegration" of personality.[10] For Laing, then, such actions represent a conscious attempt to secure one's autonomy by retreating from the threatening world of others.

While agreeing that, at times, we all experience some degree of dissociation, James put the case somewhat differently in his *Varieties of Religious Experience*. "All of us," James explained, "however constituted, but to a degree the greater in proportion as we are intense and sensitive and subject to diversified temptations," experience inward division of some sort. James, however, divided the self across its "higher and lower feelings" and "useful and erring impulses," implying that the struggle between apparently different selves emerges primarily from within a moral or spiritual drama.[11] And as one who claimed a religious import for his pragmatist perspective, James was more interested in how this experience perfects individuals than he was in its mentally debilitating implications.

For James, moreover, the phenomenon of a divided self potentially brings with it a more penetrating incursion into reality as a whole and a wider perspective on the world of self and others. Rather than resulting from a retreat from the other, which for Laing primarily meant a withdrawal from social reality, James saw the divided self

9. R. D. Laing, *The Divided Self,* 82–85, 43–44, 81.
10. Ibid., 43–44, 81.
11. William James, *The Varieties of Religious Experience: A Study of Human Nature,* 158. The first edition of James's *Varieties* was published as a collection of his Gifford lectures, delivered at the University of Edinburgh in 1901. Subsequent references will be given parenthetically in the text.

coming from an interior encounter with an interior other. Simply put, the other is, for James and also for Twain in certain texts, the unrecognized inner self. For both authors, the acceptance of this inner reality originated more from personal revelation rather than from personality adjustment and more from an unseen than a seen world; the impositions of the other within divide the self as it moves toward or away from full disclosure. "The appearance is that in this phenomenon something ideal, which in one sense is part of ourselves and in another sense is not ourselves, actually exerts an influence," one that, as James went on to say, may raise our "centre of personal energy" and produce "regenerative effects unattainable in other ways."[12]

Some post-Freudians, to be sure, would sympathize with James and Twain in their attempt to usefully exploit the apparent dual nature of human experience. "Quite clearly," as Laing himself believed, "authentic versions of freedom, power, and creativity can be achieved and lived out" by dissociative individuals. "Many schizoid writers and artists who are relatively isolated from the other," he acknowledged, "succeed in establishing a creative relationship with things in the world" by embodying the "figures of their phantasy."[13] James and Twain, however, were willing to risk believing that the experience of a divided self may lead to more than fantastic inventions and that the other may, after all, reflect a spiritual presence apart from social and material circumstance. This is precisely the notion that James fully developed in *Varieties,* a book that gathers his findings on other states of experiential being; however, his investigations into the divided self in his *Psychology* had implicitly begun moving toward a religious interpretation of the effects of discordant personalities.

James's descriptions of the French experiments with such personalities, primarily those findings of Janet and Charcot, along with the presentation of his own, are so detailed in his *Psychology* that one wonders whether Twain ventured beyond the pages of his friend's book for his references. However, both Twain and James would have known about a wide variety of experiments and other research into altered states of consciousness through their joint interest in paranormal psychology or, using its nineteenth-century name, psychical

12. Ibid., 158–59, 467.
13. Laing, *Divided Self,* 95.

research. In the writing of his dreamy tale of platonic commingling, a tale that suggests the possibility of a separate life within, Twain relied on his own continuing research into extraordinary mental manifestations as well as that of James and his colleagues in the Society for Psychical Research.

The Society for Psychical Research (S.P.R.), founded in England in 1882, represented an eclectic group of investigators into the paranormal that ranged from the spiritually inclined F. W. H. Myers, one of its founders, to the scientifically inclined Freud, one of its members in the earlier part of the twentieth century. In his essay "What Psychical Research Has Accomplished," James, who founded the S.P.R.'s American branch in 1884 and served as its president in 1894, explained that the society was formed to study that "unclassified residuum" of experience "recorded under the name of divinations, inspirations, demoniacal possessions, apparitions, ecstasies, [or] miraculous healings." Unclassifiable by "academic and critical minds," the reality of such phenomena nonetheless could be found, as James claimed, "lying broadcast over the surface of history." James and his fellow researchers, moreover, wanted to loosen the absolute grip of science, which, in its "ignorance of whole ranges and complexity" of existent phenomena, seeks to determine experiential knowledge.[14] Being just as ambivalent about the facts of science as James was, Twain too would argue for the need to inquire into the truths of personal experience of the extraordinary.

Twain accepted an offer of membership into the S.P.R. in 1884 in a letter the society chose to publish the same year in the first volume of its *Journal*.[15] By his own account, he had been a constant reader of the society's literature from its beginnings, and with his article "Mental Telegraphy," published in 1891 though mostly written in 1878, he joined his efforts with those of the society in "convincing the world that mental telepathy is not a jest."[16] Confronting similar criticism to what James countered in his own defense of psychical research, Twain chided the *North American Review* for refusing to publish his initial attempt at describing telepathic experiences. His

14. William James, "What Psychical Research Has Accomplished," 26–29.
15. Twain's letter was published in the *Journal of the Society for Psychical Research,* October 1884, as "Mark Twain on Thought-Transference," 166–67. My appendix B provides this text in its entirety.
16. Mark Twain, "Mental Telegraphy," 96.

"desire that the public should receive the thing seriously," as Twain headnoted his article, prompted his request for its anonymous publication; however, the desire of the *Review* to be taken seriously itself, as its editor explained, required its acknowledging Twain as the author.[17]

By 1891, though, Twain believed that even the odd experiences of America's acclaimed humorist would be taken seriously in the "flood of light recently cast upon mental telepathy by the intelligent labors of the Psychical Society."[18] That illuminating tide of information would have come primarily through the society's meetings and its journal, both of which had offered discourse on "thought-transference" and on cases of "clairvoyance," "double consciousness," and, important for the purposes of this study, a lengthy review of James's *Psychology*.[19]

Frederick Myers, a reviewer and friend of both James and Twain, wasted little time in connecting James's psychology to his own and to the work of psychical research in general. Concentrating on those chapters centering around the extraordinary manifestations of consciousness, Myers convincingly tied James's speculations to his own more spiritualistic perspective and, in particular, to his belief in the supernormal powers of the "subliminal self." This is Myers's own term for what psychologists would later call the subconscious.[20] As with Twain's use of the word *training,* I prefer to use the nineteenth-century terms available to Twain and James. The "subliminal" is a metaphor both men understood through their work in the S.P.R.; in his *Varieties,* James used the term frequently to describe that state of being just beyond the margins of conscious awareness. The terms *unconscious* and *subconscious* were being used in the late nineteenth century, but their definitions were somewhat vague and hence the words were used interchangeably to mean any thoughts not normally recollected in the waking state. Freud would eventually divide such latent knowledge into a "preconscious" and "unconscious" type, with

17. Ibid., 97–98.
18. Ibid.
19. Here are a few of the titles taken from the published *Proceedings* of 1891–1892: "Experimental Studies in Thought-Transference," "On the Evidence for Clairvoyance," and "A Case of Double Consciousness."
20. Myers's review of James's *Principles* is found in the *Proceedings of the Society for Psychical Research,* 1891–1892.

the former capable of erupting into the conscious mind with unusu-al force. Twain and James, however, would have been more familiar with Myers's similar notion of a subliminal "uprush" of thought, and his metaphor of the subliminal self, which suggested a rising of inward vision and mental power, provided them with a term more enabling and encompassing of religious experience.

Although Twain was an avid reader of the society's pamphlets, in which Myers continued to develop his idea of the subliminal during the early 1890s, there is no evidence to prove he read Myers's arti-cles. James, however, claimed that Myers's "theoretic work" offered the strongest link to psychology's "religious importance," which sug-gests his own close reading.[21]

Both Twain and James had been members of the S.P.R. since its formative years, and though their 1892 visit in Florence was their first recorded social meeting, the mental climate of the S.P.R. had provided them with an intellectual meeting place for quite some time. Even more, their thinking upon the nature of the self, especially as it was emerging in the 1890s, was developing within a similar psychol-ogy, one that was moving increasingly in a spiritualist direction.

James never denied the religious implications of either his psy-chology or his philosophy. "Religion is the great interest of my life," he confided to a friend in 1897.[22] However, instead of evangelical claims to the truth of religion, he preferred to speculate on the nature of the truth of experience. Although his earlier psychological and philosophical works may only hint at his "great interest," his major work, *The Varieties of Religious Experience: A Study in Human Nature,* explicitly ties his psychology to his religion. His "inquiry" was to "be psychological," as James explained while introducing the subject matter of his *Varieties*: "not religious institutions, but rather religious feelings and religious impulses" (*Varieties,* 12).

James had been inquiring into similar "feelings" and "impulses" since becoming a member of the S.P.R. and had been writing about them at least since his *Psychology* (1890). His chapter there titled "The Stream of Thought" sparks his later spiritual provocations even while it appears to restrict the boundaries of consciousness to a subjective

21. Letter to Henry W. Rankin, Newport, R.I., February 1, 1897. In James, *Letters,* 1:57. Myers's lengthy article on "The Subliminal Consciousness" can be found in its entirety in the *Proceedings of the Society for Psychical Research,* 1892.
22. James, *Letters,* 1:58.

flux of associative interests. A primary feature of our subjective streams, James pointed out in this key chapter of his *Psychology,* is that in a "penumbral nascent way," we are aware of a "fringe of unarticulated affinities," or a "halo of felt relations," accompanying the movement of thought. The fluctuation of these "psychic overtone[s]" within this movement, as fringe elements pleasurably intermingle, allows us to experience "relations and objects only dimly perceived" and to fill the gap left by our verbal limitations (*Psychology,* 1:258–59). The importance of James's idea of "fringe relations" to his theory of the "stream of consciousness" cannot be underestimated as it ultimately developed into his own argument for the truth of religious experience.

Eugene Taylor, in his reconstruction of James's 1896 Lowell lectures, argues for just such a "historical and conceptual link between psychology and religion."[23] In the Lowell lectures, James offered the fruit of his investigative research into those extraordinary manifestations of the mind so intriguing to S.P.R. members. The lectures themselves read like an update of the S.P.R. investigations; understandably, James pointed to Myers's concept of the "subliminal" as one of the society's most important contributions. Praising the work of Myers and other paranormal researchers in his 1890 article on "The Hidden Self," James pointed to the centrality of their explorations to the emerging field of psychology. "A comparative study of the trances and subconscious states is meanwhile of the most urgent importance for the comprehension of our nature."[24]

Yet Myers's description of subliminal activity, in particular, only reiterates and expands upon James's earlier attempts in the *Psychology* to articulate his theory of penumbral relations. Myers suggested the existence of at least two mental streams and that both in "continuous connection" may be "actively conscious" in "some kind of [inward] coordination" thereby forming one's "total individuality."[25] Although the James of the Lowell lectures appeared reluctant to posit

23. Eugene Taylor, *William James on Exceptional Mental States: The 1896 Lowell Lectures,* 12.
24. William James, "The Hidden Self," 373. James in fact predated Myers in describing the subliminal self in this article, which was published soon after his *Psychology.* In this essay, James felt more at will to follow his speculations on the spiritual dimensions of mind.
25. As quoted in Taylor, *Exceptional Mental States,* 42.

separate streams, he nonetheless accepted the possibility of subliminal surges bringing forth insights that transcend normal understanding. However, a few years later in his *Varieties,* James would go even further, allowing that the "subconscious self," by then a "well-accredited psychological entity" signifying the subliminal, provided the "mediating term" for signaling divine experience (457–58). James even suggested that "if there be higher spiritual agencies that can directly touch us," the "dreamy Subliminal" may provide their only means of doing so (223).[26]

James praised Twain for his brilliant use of subliminal power and "first class originality of intellect" in his 1896 Lowell lectures. James's lecture "Genius" emphasized respect for Twain's work and recognized his extraordinary creative insight.[27] During the 1890s, Twain too had ushered his psychical interests to the foreground as he increasingly turned toward fictional explorations of the psyche and toward those religious experiences that would be more clearly articulated a few years later in James's *Varieties.* Working on his *Personal Recollections of Joan of Arc* for much of the early 1890s and early drafts of the *Mysterious Stranger Manuscripts* later in the decade, Twain revealed much of that exceptional genius of which James felt him capable. Both works reflect, more explicitly than his *Adventures of Huckleberry Finn,* Twain's own developing research and his experimental attempts at fictionally expressing religious experiences. Chief among these was his experience of the divided self or the divisions within consciousness through which James, too, had been working over the same decade and across the turn of the century.

Twain also attempted to solve this enigma of duality on his own terms within his fiction; it was during the early drafting of his tale of the mysterious stranger in 1898 that he came, according to a notebook entry, to a tentative resolution. Echoing his own theorizing upon the subject in "My Platonic Sweetheart," Twain spoke of a quite distinct third self, "a spiritualized self" that he only "dimly" perceived,

---

26. In *The Mind of the Novel,* Bruce Kawin connects this Jamesian notion of subliminal activity to the experience of the "ineffable," knowing directly apprehended across or outside linguistic barriers, and realigns the subliminal within a more modern perspective on the spiritual dimensions of left- and right-brain activity.

27. Taylor, *Exceptional Mental States,* 159–60.

though he was confident that he and it shared a "common memory."[28] We shall see that it is the subliminal world of dreams that allows Twain's "spiritualized body" to freely roam. Although he attempted to construct a theory explaining his own creative process within the fluctuations of a triadic self, he never distinguished the workings of the dream self from the flights of the spiritual self; neither did he clarify their place within personal consciousness. To complicate matters further, Twain concluded his fictional theorizing by dramatically immortalizing both the dream and the spiritualized self in a final separation from the body. With the nature of the subject so complex, Twain would need more than notebook entries for his own psychic satisfaction. James posited similar relations between distinctly felt selves, or separate interlacing streams of thought, as a kind of preconscious that is within what he called the penumbral constitutive activity of the mind. Twain's brief characterization of subliminal machinations reveals his own conscious attempt to articulate those ineffable relations. In making these attempts, Twain began to resolve the enigma of self by subsuming such an idea of affinitive mental streams with an essentially religious psychology.

Before following Twain into this territory, however, we need a working definition of religion derived from both authors. Neither Twain nor James accepted religion on traditional terms; their individualism, with its emphasis on the truth of personal experience, countered what they saw as institutional abuses. Twain tucks some of his most important remarks on religion into a 1901 essay on patriotism. For Twain, patriotism is a religion, and as with any religion, it should be "reasoned out" and "fire-assayed and tested and proved" in the privacy of one's "own conscience." One should "arrange his religion so that it perfectly satisfies his conscience," Twain pointed out, not caring "whether the arrangement is satisfactory to anyone else" but himself. What is even more important, in Twain's view, is that one must refuse to accept beliefs on "command" and should instead work to "manufacture" his own religion in the "privacy and independence" of his own thoughts. Religion, in other words, is to be shaped within individual "heads and hearts," and not to be forced upon the same by coercive institutional force.[29]

---

28. Twain, *Notebook,* 350.
29. Mark Twain, "As Regards Patriotism," 476–78.

In his *Varieties,* James pointed to a similar autonomous experience as the proving grounds of religion:

> Religion, therefore, as I ask you now to arbitrarily take it, shall mean for us *the feelings, acts, and experiences of individual men in their solitude, so far as they apprehend themselves to stand in relation to whatever they may consider divine.* Since the relation may be either moral, physical, or ritual, it is evident that out of religion in the sense in which we take it, theologies, philosophies, and ecclesiastical organizations may secondarily grow. (36, James's emphasis)

At first glance, James's statement appears to leave us abstractly adrift; the "divine," like its correlating term *religion,* requires explanation as well. But James delivered. "We must interpret the term 'divine' broadly," he suggested, as "denoting any object that is god*like,* whether it be a concrete deity or not" (38). And confronted with the vagueness of yet another "floating general," James narrowed his godlike divine to the "primal reality" or necessary truth to which an "individual feels impelled to respond to solemnly and gravely" (42).

Solemn and *grave* seem dangerous adjectives to introduce to any study of Mark Twain. Certainly I do not wish to deny Twain or his readers the gaiety that often impelled Twain and pervaded his writing. In fact I wish to acknowledge the importance of that laughter that he, himself, saw as demolishing "shams and delusions," which, when taken for reality, preclude actual experience.[30] Twain's dark laughter exposes the heart of that "reality" by uncovering its faulty construction and illusory content. Within this dismantling laugh, Twain made a serious attempt to locate and negotiate the actual or "primal" condition of being and to provide an artistic design for re-creating that condition within and upon his textual world.

As with Twain, private experience lies at the heart of James's theory of religion, in which religion functions as a part of this inner experience rather than as a force acting upon it from without. For James, religion is intensely personal and functions both as a mediator of experience and as experience itself. As James said in his *Psychology,* religion provides the means of coalescing the self with the divine across an ever-shifting felt fringe of psychic relations. As

30. Mark Twain, "The Chronicle of Young Satan," 166–67.

we study Twain's own version of the religious psychology of the divided self and how he expressed this relational nature of the divine within thought's stream, we will discover that James provides us with the necessary vocabulary for interpreting the complex and often unexpected turns of Twain's mind and texts.

My intention to use James to interpret Twain requires me to clarify my own critical concerns and methodology. On one level, I am arguing a case for direct influence. A personal relationship did exist between the two men. Not only did the meeting in Florence intimately seal the bonds of friendship, as the two conversed and dined at their leisure, but there is also evidence showing a continuing personal interchange over time. The Society for Psychical Research offered years of intellectual acquaintance; both men were members from its beginnings. Both men wrote to each other, described one another in letters to others, and kept personal notes about each other in workbooks, notebooks, and copy texts. They were bonded politically as mugwumps (disenchanted Republicans who placed independent thought over party allegiance); also, as members of the Anti-Imperialist League, they united their voices against their country's imperialistic maneuvers.

Just as their first recorded meeting began, their last one ended: across the dinner table. This final dinner, in January 1907, took place after James had given the last of his Lowell Institute Lectures on pragmatism at Columbia. Following this dinner, James wrote to his brother Henry that though Twain is now "only good for monologue, in his old age," he remains a "dear little genius all the same." While the tone of his letter suggests a certain patronizing pity, James might also have been expressing his own sense of loss rather than his sorrow over Twain's apparently debilitated condition. James wrote to his brother that he had "lunched, dined, [and] breakfasted" nearly every day of his stay in New York; given his friendship with Twain, surely a few of these meals were shared with the author.[31] We can surmise, in other words, that James missed the dialogue that he and Twain had before shared.

Dialogue takes place in the wider public as well as in the narrower private domains, however. Although the two directly influenced one another on a personal level, the relation I explore is much fuller

31. James, *Letters,* 2:264.

and richer than influence alone. Both Twain and James continue to be powerful reflectors of their times; their lives covered similar historical ground and ended in the same year. They were enough like one another in attitude and agendas of concern that they belonged to the same intellectual universe; however, they were still different enough to be mutually illuminating when we read one in the light of the other. James's wealth of friends and professional acquaintances; his professionally diverse status as psychologist, philosopher, and religious theorist; and his obsessive interest in current affairs as registered in his rich display of anecdotal "clippings" argue, in themselves, for his aid in widening our lens into nineteenth-century thought. In short, his work provides a holistic reflection of his culture. His greatest value as a writer may not be as a systematic philosopher, psychologist, or religious theorist, but instead as a thoughtful observer with a talent as powerful as his brother's for blotting up everything in his culture and rendering it in his writing as a clarifying mirror of his world. The ideas and phrases we find in James were flowing back and forth in the culture long before their formal publication. Twain was not only a part of this historical dialogue but, at times, was also relying on James's reflections for his own interpretive light.

Twain, of course, was avidly reading and thinking about others as well as James. In his recent study of the ideas and personalities that influenced Twain's thinking, Sherwood Cummings shows that Twain was "exquisitely sensitive to the intellectual currents of his time."[32] Connecting his intellectual development primarily to his reading of Darwin and Hippolyte Taine, Cummings reveals how Twain used his fiction as a theoretical debating site, one through which he could work through his own ontological and epistemological doubts. Responding to the "new scientific philosophy," as Cummings puts it, Twain used his fiction for analyzing and recording his "characters' environments, activities, and inner lives objectively and in detail."[33] Taine, especially, provided him and other American literary realists with a method for analyzing and depicting characters as products of external forces. Such deterministic notions surface as a philosophical issue in nearly all of Twain's major works; for example, the mechanistic view that Twain offers in *What Is Man?*, his late philosophical

32. Sherwood Cummings, *Mark Twain and Science: Adventures of a Mind*, xii.
33. Ibid., 41–42.

text, owes much of its argument to both Darwin and Taine. However, W. E. H. Lecky's *History of European Morals* provided an opposing intuitionist's perspective, one that Cummings claims was only naively held by an idealistic young Twain. Twain, however, would never entirely lose his youthful perspective and, as he matured, would actually dwell more upon intuitionism's faith in an inner power. The scientific temper of the time cannot be overlooked, of course, and Cummings's work clearly illustrates its effect upon Twain; however, Twain's own shifting philosophical positions often turned his observing mind in less defined directions.

The following pages look toward James as that cultural mirror most capable of reflecting such movements in Twain's mind and thereby of illuminating the otherness we occasionally encounter in Twain's writing. In assessing this curious and surprising side of Twain, I intend to use James to claim what Hans Robert Jauss calls our aesthetic "bill of rights" and defines as our right to a pleasurable experience within another's "horizon of expectations."[34] To approach the cognitive circle of judgments that allows us to apprehend and articulate experience at all, we must gain an initial recognition of the strange otherness, or *alterity* (Jauss's more apt term) that we encounter when interpreting the textual past. The alterity itself compels judgment upon the inexplicable, one that Jauss believes we can and must make simultaneously from our own experiential perspective and within another's framework of expectations. "The content of the horizon of one's own experience," to use Jauss's words, "must be brought into play, and mediated through the alien horizon in order to arrive at the new horizon of another interpretation." This "fusion" of horizons, as Jauss explains, "could elicit from the text the implicit point of view that was a condition for understanding the text in the first place."[35] It is my desire to reconstruct Twain's vision within its conditioning vocabulary, particularly in its religious view of the divided self, that sends me to the texts of William James. Using James as mediating agent or cultural reflector, which allows for both perceptual and historical interplay, significantly enlarges our interpretive view of Twain and broaches those potential meanings now obscure or even lost to our present understanding.

34. H. R. Jauss, "The Alterity and Modernity of Medieval Literature," 181–229.
35. H. R. Jauss, "Horizon Structure and Dialogicity," 206, 222.

Working across the historical divides of space and time, then, this book makes an interpretive attempt to bridge the cognitive gaps created by certain modern trends of interpreting Twain. We cannot, of course, participate with the past entirely on its own terms. Any attempt to do so would be foolish and critically self-defeating. However, we can effectively increase the worth of our readings by self-consciously appropriating the past's otherness; the past can be entered, as it were, if only "through a glass darkly."[36] Or, to recall the earthier words of Huckleberry Finn, though "nothing don't look natural nor sound natural in a fog," we can nonetheless begin to normalize the unfamiliar by sounding the echoes therein.[37]

The first chapter is not systematic, but rather exploratory, exemplary, and to some extent cautionary; it focuses on a reading of three major images in *Huckleberry Finn*. Although none of James's books were available to Twain during the writing of this novel, I maintain that the implied psychology of the divided self, as Twain developed it within the narrator's internal dialogue, particularly at three decisive points of action, links Twain's text to the trajectory of James's thinking. Twain's concept of an internal dialogue complicating the more important actions of his narrator echoes, as well as anticipates, James's own developing theory of consciousness. I use *echo,* here, to suggest the interaction of the ideas and images resonating along the intellectual currents of a particular time. Both Twain and James were articulating, in their differing ways, James's eventual theory of the "stream of consciousness."

In fact, in 1884, the same year that Twain published *Huckleberry Finn,* James published most of his chapter on "The Stream of Thought" in his article "On Some Omissions of Introspective Psychology." Footnoting this chapter in his *Psychology,* James acknowledges that a "good deal" of it appeared earlier in *Mind* in January 1884. In his preface to the *Psychology* as well, he explains that several chapters of his book had been previously published in *Mind,*

36. I owe this idea of self-conscious appropriation to Edward P. Nolan, who convinced me that the past was not impenetrable. As Nolan argues in his *Now Through a Glass Darkly,* Saint Paul's expression of the limits of human knowledge, one that Jauss theoretically affirms in historical terms, aptly figures any attempt to negotiate the past.

37. Mark Twain, *Adventures of Huckleberry Finn,* 100. Subsequent references will be given parenthetically in the text.

Journal of Speculative Philosophy, Popular Science Monthly, and *Scribner's Magazine.* The list reveals James's range of movement from the academic to the popular audience, a readership that would have included Twain, who had since 1881 been an avid reader of *Popular Science Monthly,* even to the extent of forwarding his subscription while vacationing in Europe.[38]

Although I am not insisting on any direct contact between the writers at this early date, though their concurrent membership in the Society for Psychical Research implicitly allows for the possibility, I am suggesting that by reading back through James's *Psychology,* and even on toward his *Varieties,* we can begin mapping out Twain's theoretical constructions as they develop within his novel of consciousness. Not only will James's writing provide a useful language for dealing with a critical shift in perspective and a turning toward the theoretical center of Twain's own point of view, but it will provide a clarifying interpretive line across those alterities found in Twain's emergent psychology.

Twain systematically foreclosed on our desire to settle upon the meaning of his novel's central relationships. For example, many critics question Huck's part in a friendship that appears, ultimately, to deny Jim due devotion. While Twain's narrative undoubtedly explores the nature of human intimacy between Huck and Jim, encouraging competing interpretations, it can also be seen as a means of exploring the processes of Huck's own stream of thought. Twain's narrative can be usefully read as a kind of proving ground for James's thinking, as it is for Twain's own, especially as that thinking explores the workings of consciousness. My reading of Twain against James, then, leads to a hypothetical revisioning of the central relationship in the novel. Jim's presence registers upon Huck's consciousness as other, and Huck's internal confirmation of Jim's otherness rises out of his most memorable inward struggle. The story enabled Twain to present an inward encounter with another felt presence, which both he and James would eventually describe as the essence of religious experience.

My middle chapter examines the ways in which Twain manipulates our expectations in his *Personal Recollections of Joan of Arc,* a devotional hagiography that critics, for the most part, have failed to

---

38. Gribben, *Mark Twain's Library,* 554.

consider seriously.[39] Perhaps this lack of consideration stems from critics' uneasiness about Twain's depiction of Joan's "voices," arguably her central religious experience, and also from the critics' general view of Joan as an overly sentimental portrait of a saint and Victorian woman. Displaying his own uneasiness, George Bernard Shaw set the critical tone in 1924 by describing Twain's Joan as a "beautiful and most ladylike Victorian," one "skirted to the ground" and as "unimpeachable" as an "American school teacher in armor." Yet "being the work of a man of genius," as Shaw said, hedging his judgment, considering Twain's work, his Joan "remains a credible human goodygoody in spite of her creator's infatuation."[40] Whether believable or not, such a glowing portrait still evokes a disdainful critical response and may in fact trigger our own resistance to Twain's text.

As readers in our own time, we may well flinch at both fourteenth- and nineteenth-century readings of Joan of Arc, but Twain nonetheless critically challenges such a modern response. James Cox typifies the tone of standard restricted criticism when claiming that *Joan of Arc* is "so dismal as to make one wish it were a parody," and that its author is "so serious that he cannot be Mark Twain." Cox's Mark Twain, in other words, would never submit himself to the reverent endorsement of those "conventional values" lining the pages of *Joan of Arc*.[41] The project of understanding how and why he did this will be substantially aided by consideration of Twain's appropriations from William James's *The Principles of Psychology*.

Joan's pattern of submission, in particular, perplexes the modern mind and denies Twain's novel an appreciative audience. She submits to the claims of her country, through unwavering patriotism; to the laws of the Church, through papal devotion; and, most baffling of all, she acquiesces to the sacrificial demands made by her mysterious voices. We waver in front of a Twain so unabashedly proclaiming the virtues of self-denial at the command of self-proclaimed authorities. But within the perspective of nineteenth-century Ameri-

39. Susan K. Harris's *Mark Twain's Escape from Time: A Study of Patterns and Images* and J. D. Stahl's *Mark Twain, Culture and Gender: Envisioning America through Europe* provide notable exceptions to the general lack of serious consideration.

40. In the preface to George Bernard Shaw, *Saint Joan: A Chronicle Play in Six Scenes and an Epilogue*, 25.

41. James M. Cox, *Mark Twain: The Fate of Humor*, 263–64.

can sentimental fiction, as Twain's novel may fruitfully show, such self-submission can empower as well as imperil the self.

I see no reason to separate Twain entirely from those domestic novelists that, as Jane Tompkins usefully shows, idealized the "Christian tradition of self denial," one that promises Phoenix-like transformation into an ideal self from the ashes of an unregenerate one. Tompkins points out, for example, Harriet Beecher Stowe's providing a "dazzling exemplar" of "America's religion of domesticity" in *Uncle Tom's Cabin* and offering a "brilliant redaction" of nineteenth-century America's "favorite story about itself—the story of salvation through motherly love." The popularity of Stowe's novel could not have escaped Twain—both he and Stowe were a part of the Hartford literary circle at Nook Farm—and the relationship Jim and Huck share aboard the raft partakes at times of a similar "religion," Huck finding a saving or regenerative experience through the love of a "motherly" Jim. But the habit of self-denial necessary for re-creating the self comes only through what many called "training," and, as Tompkins explains, the domestic novelists felt it their responsibility to promote such habitual behavior.[42]

Reading Twain as an advocate of behavioral training, especially as a moralist advocating self-discipline, certainly threatens any easy attempt to reveal Twain as an advocate of freedom in *Huckleberry Finn*. However, *freedom* for Twain meant something other than just escaping from moral responsibility; its experience follows from a struggle to comprehend and appropriate the truth of that responsibility on one's own terms. The act of such an appropriation then enables a "funding" of personal freedom through a choice to believe and to act upon one's own realization of the truth.

This *funding of freedom* thematically grounds my critical project in Jamesian terms. James's own use of the term *funding* can best be read as reflecting his idea of truth. Truth is continually in process for James; experiences are made true when we invest ourselves in them. Acting upon belief pushes it forward as experiential fact and verifies its existence. Freedom, then, means believing in our capacity to expe-

---

42. Jane Tompkins, *Sensational Designs: The Cultural Work of American Fiction, 1790–1860*, 125, 175, 176. In his *Sentimental Twain: Samuel Clemens in the Maze of Moral Philosophy*, Gregg Camfield expands upon Tompkins's project as he recovers the moral and intellectual underpinnings of American sentimentalism and establishes Twain's role as literary sentimentalist.

rience freedom itself; acting upon our belief creates the possibility of realizing the experience. Like other experiences, as James maintained, freedom happens like an event.[43] The capacity for such an experience, however, requires the effort of both a hero and a saint to direct and reenvision both thought and action. Here I turn again to James's discussion of "habit" in chapter 4 of the *Psychology*, a chapter that Twain read and commented on and that helps clarify an otherwise surprising Twain.

Saintliness is possible, as James explained in that chapter, only through acquiring "habits of attention, energetic volition, and self-denial" (1:127). All these promote a healthy will and decisive heroic action, according to James, rather than that "miserable human" condition of "indecision" (1:122). Adhering to James's notions, Twain depicted his Joan as habitually training her will to respond independently of her initial, primordial desires. Twain's portrayal of the divided self places those desires in opposition to the awakened will. The training of the will situates Joan's voices at yet another level of consciousness. Whereas with Huck no integration within consciousness is possible as he deliberately directs his actions in spite of the force of his thinking, Joan appears to integrate her own will with that of her inner voices of authority, even as she negates any other self that might stand apart from each.

James also made some important observations about the necessity of self-submission in his *Varieties*. "The constitution of the world we live in requires it," he explains, "for when all is said and done, we are absolutely dependent on the universe" and are of necessity drawn into "sacrifices and surrenders of some sort" (53). Religion becomes vitally important, then, for making "easy and felicitous what in any case is necessary," and indeed, James suggests it is an "essential organ of our life, performing a function which no other portion of our nature can so successfully fulfill" (53). Religion enables us to accept the universe on its own conditions, in James's psychology, and the self-negating experiences of religion in them-

43. William James, *Pragmatism: A New Name for Some Old Ways of Thinking,* ed. Bruce Kuklick, 101. *Pragmatism* was published as a collection of James's Columbia lectures of 1907. It seems probable that Twain attended these lectures, since he and other friends of James's celebrated their success at a dinner given in James's honor. Subsequent references to *Pragmatism* will be given parenthetically in the text.

selves offer true salvation from inevitable suffering. And regardless of its anterior publication date, the *Varieties* throws helpful light upon Twain's own fictional investigations into religious experience. In fact, the light shines back upon both Twain and James as in the 1890s they both increasingly turned their thoughts toward the phenomena of religious experiences.

In the final chapter, I show how these experiences take on a fictive life in Twain's *No. 44* and theoretical force in James's *Varieties*. James, true to his definition of religious experience, centered his *Varieties* on a host of testimonies to the reality of the experiential divine, that is, the felt presence inwardly impelling solemn reflection. His subtitle, *A Study in Human Nature,* points both to this inward reflection and to a study of human nature in general, revealing his work to be a psychology and philosophy of religion—though a good dose of philosophy always filters through any Jamesian psychology. In these terms, Twain's *No. 44* may be seen as embodying a similar psychology. Twain's text could certainly share James's subtitle as it careens along the corridors of narrative consciousness and toward self-disclosure; its narrator's own multiple experiences of inward divinity defer to more than a few of James's own examples. Moreover, as Twain leads us into the textual center of his work, his psychology emerges in Jamesian terms as yet another description of religious experience, one predicating the self as other and the other self as divine.

Twain's marks and comments in the margins of his personal copy of James's *Varieties* reveal his own struggle with doubt and uncertainty even as he was writing *No. 44,* a text that ultimately concludes on an affirmative note. I believe that the intellectual participation revealed in Twain's marginalia provides further evidence for reading Twain within the particular vocabulary of William James.[44] Although the last chapter draws upon Twain's comments and markings within his copy of the *Varieties,* it does not focus on them exclusively. By the time Twain finished his *No. 44* in 1908, all the relevant texts of James were available to him. He had read and commented upon

44. Twain's copy of James's *Varieties* is in the private collection of Judge Harry Pregerson, United States Court of Appeals, Los Angeles, Calif. I wish to formally thank him for allowing me to cite from a copy of this text.

James's *Principles* and his *Varieties*. Also, his dining with James and others who had attended the final Columbia lecture on pragmatism, one in which James fused his philosophy into a melioristic religion, strongly suggests that Twain had heard, if not read, James's views upon the subject for which he remains best known. Outside this textual interchange, their mutual interest in the paranormal that brought them together in the Society for Psychical Research provides a crucial link between both the *Varieties* and *No. 44*.

Like the *Varieties, No. 44* looks to the theoretical constructions of the subconscious for its religious psychology and for its effectiveness in explaining exceptional experiences. Twain's narrative becomes a fictional workshop for many such experiences upon which he and James, along with most members of the S.P.R., had been speculating since the 1880s. Theories on dreams, hypnotism, and hallucinations as well as on clairvoyancy, mental telepathy, and multiple personalities stream through Twain's fictional excursion into the subliminal life of his narrator, August Feldner.

Little wonder that *No. 44* continues to baffle critics. Huck's moral heroism is undeniable, and Joan of Arc conjures up Promethean actions defining heroism itself. Yet with Twain's choice of August Feldner as the narrator-protagonist of *No. 44,* Twain's traditional marks of heroism appear disturbingly absent. We find ourselves pressing against the limits of our own expectations. August can even be read as embodying a mind of excessive passivity and moral sloth, generally the target of Twain's sharpest satire.

August fits in with Huck and Joan, however, in a growing literary epistemological drama that warrants fresh exploration. Played out upon the stage of consciousness, Twain's characters struggle within their own limits of knowledge, sifting through belief, doubt, and faith while forging ahead beyond recognizable boundaries. They move forward as pioneers in that continual flow of thought that James called the stream of consciousness; on this perpetual frontier, they risk self-abnegation as they encounter and build upon self-discovery. For Twain this meant the discovery of a different self; for the characters that lead us through this "mental drama" (James's phrase), it means a discovery of their heroic potential; and for readers, it reveals the possibility of reconfiguring perception.

Reading this interior drama against James's reflections in *The Varieties of Religious Experience* helps us mediate our experience with our expectations. It is an essentially religious struggle, according to James, and carries its participant into a "new sphere of power," one that "redeems and vivifies an interior world which would otherwise be an empty waste" (*Varieties,* 50). One who emerges victoriously from such an inward journey is, in Jamesian/Twainian terms, a hero. As readers sharing the characters' perception, experiencing the struggle may mean, to recast James's words, "nothing short of [a] new reach of freedom for us" (*Varieties,* 50). James's "new reach of freedom" can be taken to mean nothing short of a partaking of divine creativity itself. Like James, Twain crafted his own literary psychology in order to show the possibility of releasing the self from the exigencies of internal division into the creative empowerment of divine cooperation.

Mark Twain's art and mind challenge all who attempt to understand his central ideas, those strands of thought forming the philosophical core of his vision. Yet as Stanley Brodwin reminds us before making his own attempt to illuminate the "profounder dimensions" of Twain's psyche, we must meet the challenge "in the expectation that any judgment we make" about an author, even in the face of "radical contradictions," will "yield us a measure of consistency in all the inconsistencies we are bound to discover."[45] In revisioning Twain as entering into the liminal territory that religion shares with ontology, epistemology, and freedom, I found myself particularly enmeshed in an eclectic, at times inconsistent, body of facts and fictions, beliefs and principles, theories and theologies. Yet Twain's intricate blending of this diverse body of knowledge, however complex or seemingly incompatible the mix, offers to delight and surprise his readers.

This book, then, uses the work of William James to provide some degree of consistency for understanding and appreciating Twain's rarer side. It also offers to lead its readers to a more critically satisfying perspective on Twain's life work. James enables us not only to accept that work in a new light, but also to enjoy more fully the strangeness of encountering Twain at the most mysterious junctures of his literary career.

45. Stanley Brodwin, "Mark Twain's Theology," 220. In this definitive essay, Brodwin maps the core ideas behind Twain's religious aesthetic.

— 1 —
Developing the Introspective Link
Adventures of Huckleberry Finn

I couldn't tell nothing about voices in a fog, for nothing don't look natural nor sound natural in a fog.
— Mark Twain, *Adventures of Huckleberry Finn*

*T*his chapter recognizes what for many will be another Twain as it begins to locate his thought and language within the theoretical purview of William James. While his *Adventures of Huckleberry Finn* displays the apex of Twain's rich sense of humor, it simultaneously reveals a more sober, speculative play of mind in the novel's exploration of consciousness. Twain's literary excursion into this interior realm has yet to be fully examined; by tracing the reflections of James, we can begin to extrapolate more fully Twain's early speculations on the workings of consciousness, especially as he played them out within the internal dialogues of Huck Finn. Within the interior river dialogues we move from Twain's social concern to the individual's struggle for personal freedom, the narrative's central concern.

As James theorized upon this mental "stream of thought," the flux of consciousness as we sense or experience it, Twain figured his hero's self-liberating moves through a complex and often conflicting interior flow of relations as Huck and Jim drift over the surface of the Mississippi River. Both writers rejected the image of consciousness as a train or chain of discrete ideas, preferring instead to describe it as a river or a "stream of thought, of consciousness, or of subjective life."[1] To James this description was crucial for his theory of relations and transitions, those felt phenomena that keep truth and meaning in flux within the whole stream of experience. It was equally crucial for Twain, who was still working through the epistemological difficulties of his theory of consciousness. Neither author was particularly systematic—though James could be more so than Twain when called upon—so the early theorizing of Twain and James resists definitive framing, yet always implies more to come. An initial look at some Jamesian reverberations in *Huckleberry Finn* opens the subject of self and consciousness and will help us better anticipate the later theorizing of both men, especially in the areas of inquiry surrounding subliminal regions of thought.

Three famous scenes in the novel illuminate Twain's developing psychology as he grappled with perceived divisions within the mind. Chief among these divisions is the tension he felt existed between the natural and the supernatural or the material and the spiritual. Twain initially projected this duality in chapter 15 where Huck, separated from Jim, finds/loses himself in a fog of strange, unearthly voices. Keeping interior dialogue to a minimum here, Twain helps Huck resist the sense of inclusiveness of being that the whole experience suggests is growing within the relationship developing aboard the raft. The narrative's emphasis, however, has begun to shift toward a study of Huck's mind; by setting the scene within the context of Twain's interest in psychical research, together with the thinking of William James, we shall better understand it as a precursor to Twain's later and more sustained depictions of extraordinary states of mind.

Chapter 16 reveals Huck's deep ambivalence in the face of a desired, yet feared, inclusivity that unites him and Jim against the world by means of his famous lie ("He's white"), a lie that indicates his astonishing sensitivity as well as his growing love for Jim. The point of view now shifts radically if tentatively at this point, as Twain now directs our attention to Huck's interior reflections. Such reflections point outside the text to Twain's own struggle with the problem of human freedom and to his perspective on the dual and determin-

---

1. James, *The Principles of Psychology*, 1:239. James's metaphor points to what he believed to be lacking in psychological research, the description of felt experience. James began developing his own reflections on the continuous flow of experience as early as 1884 and the publication of "On Some Omissions of Introspective Psychology."

istic nature of mind. Reading Twain's ideas against the notions of
William James, who was working toward a like philosophy of mind,
provides us with a clarifying angle of vision, an opening view into
Twain's concept of a divided self.

Another interior turn dominates chapter 31, as Huck settles the
issue of freedom, both his and Jim's, by willing it out to the world
from within the core of his nature. Turning here toward the intellectual context of Twain's developing "soft" determinism and its allow-
ance for a "soul," or a creative inmost center, allows us to see that
Huck's decision to liberate Jim through his own choice of hell frees
his own thinking for that indeterminate play of thought, to recast
James's words, that allows the mind to actualize possibilities.[2] The
interrelations that emerge across these scenes are often loose, partial,
and imprecise, if not contradictory; relying upon his own introspection, Twain himself was still in the process of thinking through his
psychology.

As we read his thoughts against James's wider-ranging theory of
consciousness, however, we see them begin to take on a more coherent shape. The psychology of both Twain and James derives shape
as much from their philosophy and their thinking upon the human
condition and its essential nature as from direct observation of human
behavior. Moreover, the dilemma posed by the desire for freedom, in
the face of an apparently cosmic determinism, thematically engaged
the minds of both Twain and James and provided them with the
philosophical nexus necessary for constructing similar psychologies.
The theories of both were built primarily in response to their reluc-
tance to accept determinism's compelling argument. Their ontological and epistemological forays into this central philosophical conun-
drum were part of their lifelong attempts to seize the truth about the
issue; their process deserves close scrutiny. Twain's fictional theorizing upon consciousness, or the concept of self, emerges from the
implied dialectic of determinism and free will pervading his fiction.

Maintaining Freedom's Possibility

Twain lightly introduces the deterministic argument in one of his

2. William James, "The Dilemma of Determinism," in *The Will to Believe, and Other Essays in Popular Philosophy,* 182–84.

novel's most humorous scenes, one in which we find Jim responding to Huck's defense of Solomon's wisdom. Jim thinks he knows better, however, and sets Huck straight recalling Solomon's most famous decision "bout dat chile he 'uz gwyne to chop in two." As Jim figures, Solomon believed children to be of little worth, since he probably had "five million" of them "runnin' roun de house," and he would as "soon chop a chile in two as a cat." When Huck protests Jim's missing the point, Jim offers his own brand of wisdom: "Blame de pint! I reck'n I knows what I knows. En mine you, de *real* pint is down furder—it's down deeper. It lays in de way Sollermun was raised" (94–96).[3] Concerning Solomon and his wisdom, Jim's understandings may be a bit cloudy, but they come to haunt Huck and his narrative as he finds himself mentally wrestling toward his own freedom.

Mark Twain and William James, unlike Huck, would have no problem accepting Jim's reasoning—with qualifications. They devoted much time and paper to exploring "down furder" and, like Jim, were deeply engaged in observing the effects of training upon individual thought and action. Twain had responded to the forceful arguments of determinism well before *Huckleberry Finn* portrayed Huck's dramatic struggle with his own determining forces; in fact his early responses were made primarily in defense of deterministic claims. In 1881 and 1883 he tested his defense before the Monday Evening Club of Hartford; he introduced threads of thought that would eventually weave their way into his later "What Is Man?" His audience scoffed at the idea of the "human machine," a mechanical concept of the mind that left it incapable of generating an original idea or action apart from the governing influences of biology and culture. As he often did when confronted with similar resistance from "superior minds," Twain refrained, for the time being at least, from further speaking his own mind about the matter.[4]

Twain respected the members of Hartford's Monday Evening Club, and his deference to their informal tutelage reveals the tenta-

3. Bruce Michelson lucidly recounts Twain's own struggle toward independent thought in *Mark Twain on the Loose: A Comic Writer and the American Self*. Michelson convincingly argues that from his early travel narratives to his late fantasies, Twain strove to destabilize social and literary configurations of self in an effort to affirm its essentially anarchic freedom.

4. Mark Twain, *Mark Twain in Eruption: Hitherto Unpublished Pages about Men and Events*, 240–41.

tive nature of his early speculations and deterministic claims. The Monday Evening Club, in other words, provided Twain a setting in which to examine both his doubts and beliefs, one in which he could develop his ideas in dialogue with an eclectic group of literary intellectuals and religious thinkers. He would cowrite *The Gilded Age* with Charles Dudley Warner, one of the more literary members of the club, and through his friendship with Joseph Twichell, another club regular and minister of the liberal Congregational Church, Twain would find a sympathetic listener and influential guide for his own religious liberalism.

In considering the claims of determinism, however, Twain would turn to other influential guides. Twain's ideas about the controlling influences of culture, biology, and even race were hardly new, though such thinking had only slowly made its way across the Atlantic during the 1870s as American literary realists absorbed it primarily through the work of the French intellectual Hippolyte Taine. Taine's philosophy, as Sherwood Cummings notes as he connects it to America's realistic movement, provided Twain with a "rationale and method" for exploring the "soul" of his characters as well as that of his nation. Since character was the result of the formative forces acting upon it, according to Taine, literary characters could be known and examined through a detailed presentation of the effects of those forces within and upon them. Like other American realists—including his close friend, William Dean Howells—Twain hoped to provide an "exact divination of the inner workings of the mind and heart" (Taine's words) by opening them to literary inspection against their biological and environmental influences.[5] Much of Twain's own literary technique at this time stemmed from his reading of Taine, as Cummings persuasively argues, and his work undoubtedly reveals Taine's philosophy through the actions of his characters and within the fictional worlds of his texts.

Twain's deterministic turn was far from permanent, however. Even when declaring as he did in *Connecticut Yankee,* one of his more skeptical works, that everything depends on "heredity and training," that "we have no thoughts of our own," he acknowledged at the same time an autonomous, albeit minute, center of being. The "rest

5. Sherwood Cummings, *Mark Twain and Science: Adventures of a Mind,* 68–69.

may land in Sheol," as Twain bluntly put it, though he dedicated much of his work to saving that small particle of self he believed free, the true "me."[6] Though never wholly proclaiming the self as free, Twain held out the possibility of thinking freely, as he himself explained in 1907 upon recalling his earlier views, once "prejudices, predilections, and inheritances" had been "swept away."[7] Twain's attempts to sweep such hindrances away define much of his work as a writer, and with *Huckleberry Finn,* he not only swept a path through the intellectual encumbrances of determinism but cleared the ground for the positing of a vital force capable of functioning apart from its strictures. This meant a continual oscillation away from and back to a host of environmental determinisms even as Twain emphasized the possibility of a free will.

Twain had been speculating upon more spontaneous faculties of mind before fictionally embodying his theories in *Huckleberry Finn.* His experiences with mental telepathy in the 1870s, though not proving the freedom or even the originality of thought, certainly questioned the contextual claims of determinism. If "mind can communicate accurately with mind without the aid of the slow and clumsy vehicle of speech," as Twain suggested in his article "Mental Telegraphy," then more than the known impinges upon our thought.[8] This "more" was an enigmatic puzzle that Twain would continue piecing together all his life.

As he worked toward the publication of *Huckleberry Finn,* a book that provided an essential piece for solving this puzzle, Twain sought a psychology that could account for the nature of thought itself. In his suppositions on mental telepathy, Twain described it as the "succession of thoughts or sensations [that] flocks in upon [us]" from seemingly nowhere though with an unaccountable sense of personal authorization. It may be that "some far-off stranger has been telegraphing his thoughts and sensations into [our] consciousness," Twain further supposed, anticipating his own later account of this "hoary mystery." He theorized that investigations into these lines of

6. Mark Twain, *A Connecticut Yankee in King Arthur's Court,* 162.

7. Twain, *Mark Twain in Eruption,* 241.

8. Mark Twain, "Mental Telegraphy," 105. Twain wrote most of this essay in 1878; however, waiting for a more amenable time and place, he would not publish it until 1891.

communication will uncover the inward operations of the self.[9] As he revealed in "Mark Twain on Thought-Transference," an article published by the Society for Psychical Research (S.P.R.) within months of the publication of *Huckleberry Finn,* by 1884 his investigations into the complexities of thought and the workings of consciousness were not leading him wholeheartedly into determinism's camp.[10] Rather, Twain's early theorizing upon mental processes reveals the seeds of his later belief in the essentially indeterminate nature of thought and action. This belief eventually led to the playful freedom of the "far-off stranger" of his *Mysterious Stranger Manuscripts* and to a depiction of that liberating stranger as within but, at the same time, apart from the boundaries of self.

His early speculations also resonate with the developing theories of William James. James, too, was coming to terms with the epistemological and ontological difficulties of determinism, ones that nearly brought him to the point of mental paralysis, as he increasingly turned his attention toward that "hoary mystery" of the self. In fact, James had contemplated suicide as the only way to truly declare one's freedom; turning away from suicide, however, he resolved to "voluntarily cultivate the feeling of moral freedom" in the future through "willful choice" and "accumulated *acts* of thought," actions necessary for "salvation" itself. For the young James, life would "be built in doing and suffering and creating," a central imperative an older James continued to build upon as well.[11]

His own membership in the Society of Psychical Research underscores James's will to create and his early interests in exploring the workings of consciousness and the effectual range of the mind. James was giving a voice to his contemporaries' attempts to understand the intricate parts of the mind, whether it be in the more popular

9. Ibid., 102–3.

10. Twain's article was published in the first volume of the *Journal of the Society for Psychical Research* in October 1884 in response to the society's wish that he become a member. Accepting his membership in his article "Mark Twain on Thought-Transference," he reveals his long-standing interest in the paranormal.

11. James's cure for his own moral despondency, as he explains in a notebook entry in 1870, came through his reading of Renouvier, specifically in his choice to accept Renouvier's definition of *free will* as his own: "the sustaining of a thought *because I choose to* when I might have other thoughts." In *The Letters of William James,* 1:147–48.

soundings of the self emerging from the members of the S.P.R. or the more "respectable" sound of his own academic colleagues at Harvard. But James's voice finds a particularly provocative echo in the work of Twain and in Twain's fictional and intermittent arguments for the freedom of the will.

In his 1884 article "The Dilemma of Determinism," James professed his own belief in "indeterminism" and in the "ultimate pluralism" of the world, a belief that implicitly affirms the possibility of thinking freely; this belief finds an echo, however tentative, in the fictional form of *Huckleberry Finn*.[12] Indeterminism allows for a "certain amount of loose play" in the world, as James explained it, and that "possibilities may be in excess of actualities," possibilities that we may or may not choose to realize. "The great point is that the possibilities are *here*," as James insisted, and are decided upon "nowhere else than *here* and *now*." James realized that this choice to "believe in liberty," to believe "anything is decided here and now," is no more than just a choice to believe, but in so choosing, as James suggested, we turn belief itself into fact.[13] The point here is that for James, a choice of possibilities exists, a choice that would allow for the creative movement of an independent mind.

For James's part, his profession itself would authenticate his belief, and in his chapter entitled "Will," near the end of *Psychology,* he again reiterates his faith in the indeterminate nature of thought and action despite plaguing uncertainties:

> Doubt of this particular truth will therefore probably be open to us to the end of time, and the utmost that a believer in free-will can *ever* do will be to show that the deterministic arguments are not coercive. That they are seductive, I am the last to deny; nor do I deny that effort may be needed to keep the faith in freedom, when they press upon it, upright in the mind. (2:573–74)[14]

Although few put more "effort" into maintaining the faith than James,

12. James's essay on determinism was published while key sections of his *Psychology* were in their formative stages: "The Stream of Thought," "The Consciousness of Self," and his chapter on the "Will."

13. James, "The Dilemma of Determinism," 150–51, 183.

14. James's abundant use of italics throughout his *Psychology,* sometimes emphatically denoting whole paragraphs of information, reminds us that the book was originally published as a textbook.

Twain did his "utmost" in *Huckleberry Finn* to profess it—and it was a faith he would never entirely lose.

Twain and James, then, would only partially agree with Jim's argument concerning Solomon's wisdom. Neither would deny the influential pull of training, the whole weight of one's influencing environment, but both would deny the finality of its determining influence. Human agency had to be free if creative effort, important to both Twain and James, was to make a significant difference. And within *Huckleberry Finn* and the *Psychology,* Twain and James posit a governing center significantly differentiating itself from habitual responses, a creative locus more or less felt in the sense of grasping something even larger than the self, something ineffable yet commanding.

For Twain, positing this central axis of being, a pivotal dynamic that powered free and independent action, meant developing a psychology of a divided self. And although his *Joan of Arc* and *No. 44, The Mysterious Stranger* ultimately distinguish the self's divisions within separate levels of existence, *Huckleberry Finn* lays the groundwork for both texts, particularly in the three key scenes we may now read anew in the light of William James.

Psychical Probings and the Sting of Language:
"Dat Truck dah is Trash"

In chapter 15 and the nearly disastrous separation of Jim and Huck within the dense fog clinging to the Mississippi River, we watch as Huck mentally collides with the reality of Jim's otherness, an encounter that prefigures his later and more famous struggles with his conscience. In fact, Huck's conscience only comes into play in the concluding moments of this chapter and then only in an immediate response to the precepts of friendship, as laid down by Jim, and not to its own previously informed dictates. More to the point, Twain fused conscience and consciousness early in Huck's adventures as he began to theorize upon the inner thoughts and feelings of his hero. The chapter as a whole, redolent with dream and liminal imagery, shifts the emphasis of the novel away from the situational humor dependent on Jim's and Huck's earlier conflicting views in the teeming exterior world, toward the more complex operations arising in the interior of Twain's hero.

Twain begins this journey into his hero's psyche by opening the chapter with those reflections that would increasingly problematize Huck's image of himself. He and Jim are nearing Cairo, the doorway to Jim's freedom, and though Huck contemplates heading north toward the "free states," the confusion that ensues as fog blankets the Mississippi River both figures and reflects Huck's own mixed emotions over his part in aiding and abetting a slave and the bewildering effects of his relationship with Jim. Huck's view of Jim is slipping, sliding, and shifting within his own mind even as Jim fades into the fog bank along the Mississippi. The fog that descends upon the river metaphorically settles upon Huck's thinking stream, distancing him not only from Jim but also from any secure sense of himself.

"I shot out into the solid white fog," Huck explains, "and hadn't no more idea which way I was going than a dead man" (99). Yet, downstream, "somewheres," he "hears a small whoop" that lifts his "spirits," but "flying around, this way and that and t'other," he loses direction, unable to follow the "small" voice resounding within the fog. "Well, I fought along and directly I hears the whoop *behind* me. I was tangled good, now. That was somebody else's whoop, or else I was turned around" (100). Unsure of his direction or of that of the voices, Huck decides to just "give up" and float within the fog's echoing entourage.

Floating within the fog bank of his mind as well, Huck experiences a liminal shifting of psychic boundaries. "Floating along" and "laying dead still on the water," he drifts in and out of the "solid white" fog (100). Hearing "no sign of a whoop nowheres" and believing himself completely lost, Huck allows himself to continue to drift downstream half-awake, only to gradually awaken to the realization of his precarious situation, "spinning down a big bend stern first" (101–2). After reclaiming fragments of his identity as if from somewhere "up dim out of last week," Huck emerges from the whole experience safe yet only questionably sound (102). As the fog lifts, however, Huck realigns himself within the comfortable horizons of his former views, and the self that he re-collects exposes the same defects essentially unchanged.

He is still "jis de same ole Huck," as Jim joyously proclaims upon Huck's return through the fog and back to the raft (103). Ironically, Jim speaks more truth than he knows as his joy finds a short life with the "same ole Huck" whose self-protective fiction tramples upon

Jim's vulnerability. He convinces Jim that his suffering over their separation in the fog and the ensuing pain induced by the fear of Huck's loss had all been in vain, which compels Jim to deny the evidence of his own senses by accepting the entire disconcerting experience as a dream.

Huck learned little if anything from his disorienting experience in the fog, and has yet to clear a path through his own prejudicial haze. Clearing this path will require something more than just a momentary loss of direction and poorly directed, guilt-ridden apology; for Huck it will require nothing less than a struggle toward independent selfhood and a reshaping or redirecting of identity through an independent act of his own.

Twain's depiction of Huck's disorienting affair on the river signals a growing curiosity about a wider realm of experience and reveals that ambivalent relationship with the spiritual or supernatural that would continue to provoke Twain's thought. Alan Gribben usefully details this relationship in his essay on Twain's occult interests; Gribben suggests that a prophetic dream in 1858 about his brother's death piqued Twain's interest in the supernatural.[15] Gribben, however, fails to mention Huck's directionless floundering within the fog in his consideration of *Huckleberry Finn,* even though it is the one episode in the novel that seriously explores an experience with supernatural implications.

It is an episode that forges an important link between Twain and James as well: their membership in the S.P.R. Twain's founding membership in the American wing of the S.P.R. suggests that he, like its other most fervent members, including James, was unwilling to construct a spiritually vacant psychology. In the society's early theorizing upon the effect of dreams, the actions of the will, and the "acts of the unconscious mind," we can recognize a confluent stream of interests bent on freeing humanity from the strict impositions of scientific determinism. The society, furthermore, assumed a proactive mind, not a reactive one. The mind that perhaps more than any other provided a viable vocabulary for a spiritual psychology was that of William James. It was belief, after all, that functioned to free James's

15. Alan Gribben, "'When Other Amusements Fail': Mark Twain and the Occult," 182. Years later, Twain would try to communicate with his brother Henry, as well as his deceased daughter, through the efforts of a medium.

own thinking, a declared faith in free will; it was his thinking upon religion that would ultimately confirm such freedom and more in his *Varieties of Religious Experience: A Study in Human Nature.*

James and Twain were busy working their beliefs about human nature into their psychological theories, beliefs that would allow for the moral and religious significance of self-determination. At the same time, though, they yielded, however ambivalently, to the scientific opinion of their day, which often rejected the essentially Emersonian claim of spiritual intuition so central to American religious thought. The concept of an essentially vitalistic psychology apart from a transcendent power, yet still within the powerful framework of scientific opinion, presented Twain and James with certain metaphysical difficulties; the primary one was not only a defense of a freely creative mind but also the exposition of the thought process necessary for that mind's creative freedom. Although their more articulate response to these difficulties would come later, in their different ways Twain and James were anticipating the concepts that would connect them more closely within a shared and, to their view, viable terminology, one that to a large extent James would produce.

Huck's near-mystical experience in the fog, reflecting Twain's own psychical research, is one such anticipation; James would eventually provide the bridging vocabulary required for a discourse mediating the supernatural experiences similar to Huck's. At the conclusion of the *Varieties,* James suggests that such experiences signal an "incursion from the subconscious region," one that, in raising the "centre" of personal awareness, may validate the realization of "transmundane energies" and the existence of "a wider world of being than that of our every-day consciousness" (467). However, in the 1880s, neither Twain in his fiction nor James in his essays was ready to validate this "wider world" upon these terms, and although Twain plays with the idea of the supernatural in *Huckleberry Finn,* attempting to negotiate his speculations through the materialistic claims of science, his psychology would require a more natural, scientific grounding.

If the continued defense of an essentially indeterminate self were ever to be taken seriously, both Twain and James would need to "keep close to the point of view of natural science," as James himself declared for his own intentions in the prefatory pages of the *Psychology.* His psychology, "the science of finite individual minds," James explained, will assume no reality outside that of "thoughts and feelings" and the "physical world in time and space" in which "they coexist" and "know" (vi). To do so would represent a "metaphysical" attempt to "explain our phenomenally given thoughts as products of deeper-lying entities," the "Soul" or "Transcendental Ego" for instance. And though Twain flirts with just such an explanation early in *Huckleberry Finn,* he seems as resolved as James to be taken seriously. The nineteenth century still recognized the reality of the will as a mental faculty at least; if Twain were to seriously argue for its freedom, he would need to remain within the realm of the finite.

Twain would thus confine himself to the "scientific" study of Huck's "finite" mind as it thought and felt its way through the relations of the real world of the raft and Jim. But the problems of representing a self-fashioning mind within the confines of finite thought were not easily overcome, though Twain and James both counted upon what they believed to be commonly acknowledged mental states, ones in which feelings, thoughts, and sensations were felt as well as known, for their own theoretical credibility.

Twain and James's task, then, was to develop a psychology that would allow for viable extralinguistic experiences even within the limitations of a language-bound understanding, a psychology assuming a consciousness within a finite world but not wholly bound to it. Both men required a metaphysics as much as a psychology; they steered between material and spiritual demands as their thinking converged upon and expanded out from an enabling ontological and epistemological viewpoint. They sought and eventually provided a *via media* between science and religion in their vision of interpenetrating boundaries of experience.

James best articulated this medial perspective in his *Psychology* with a definition of "reality" which, while situating the self in the world, suggests an infinite expansion of both the self and its world. "Reality," as James wrote in his *Psychology,* "means simply relation to our emotional and active life" and, he continued, to the degree that an "object so appeals to us that we turn to it, accept it . . . or practically take account of it," to that degree it is real. Simply put, *"whatever excites and stimulates our interest is real"* (2:295). James grounded his theory of reality in the decisive weight of individual choice:

> The world of living realities . . . is thus anchored in the Ego . . .
> the hook from which the rest dangles, the absolute support . . .

> Whatever things have intimate and continuous connection with
> my life are things whose reality I cannot doubt. Whatever things
> fail to establish this connection are things which are practically
> no better for me than if they existed not at all. (2:297)

The importance of language in making this intimate connection to the
ego, as well as in engaging the emotions, lies in its ability to maintain the continuous link between objects and the ego—the link
between the world and the self:

> Reality, starting from the Ego, thus sheds itself from point to
> point—first, upon all objects which have an immediate sting of
> interest for our Ego in them, and next, upon the objects most
> continuously related with these. It only fails when the connect-
> ing thread is lost. A whole system may be real, if it only hang to
> our Ego by one immediately stinging term. (2:297)

Without being as theoretical as James, nor as ambitious to account for
the whole scheme of things, Twain develops Huck's relationship with
Jim in a way that fictively vivifies James's notion of the ego and its
objects—the self and its reality.

The "stinging" term that actualizes Jim for Huck, that allows him to
exist within the boy's mind as an undeniable reality, is the simple
word, "frens," delivered poignantly by Jim in the concluding lines of
chapter 15. Actually Jim's whole definitive analogy is shot full of
stinging terms that continue to trigger Huck's thinking; but for now it
is the word "friends" that stirs his emotions and commands his interest, weaving the crucial link between idea and reality. Jim's signaling
of what friends ought to be, or ought not to be, sets the idea of Jim,
himself, adrift in the consciousness of Huck. Although Huck is not yet
completely aware of the intimate bond he and Jim are forming or the
reality he is establishing, the "connecting thread" within tightens as
he responds to the piercing immediacy of the word "friends."

By discussing Jim as an idea or phenomenon within the consciousness of Huck, I risk losing sight of the intimacies developed
within the human relationship forming between the boy and the
slave. A study of Huck's mind, that is, may seemingly entail a nega-
tion of his outward relations with both Jim and the community at
large. Yet Huck's early separation from Jim allows Twain to begin a
study of Huck's mind; a turning inward, as Twain seems to suggest,

is precisely what may be needed for creating new relations. Richard Poirier, in his study of a peculiarly American style, believes this to be the case for particular writers, among whom he includes Twain and James. He explains that both belonged to that cadre of American writers who, carrying the "metaphoric burden" of their country's "great dream of freedom," attempted to write themselves, as well as their readers, beyond the "forces of environment that otherwise dominate the world." This meant turning inward toward those states of consciousness that, according to Poirier, defy limiting constructions; in *Huckleberry Finn* in particular, it also involved isolating the hero's consciousness in order to creatively construct a free world.[16]

Poirier points out, as I do, that in chapter 15 Twain emphatically shifts his focus to the subject of consciousness, prefiguring the liberating struggles Huck is soon to endure. He further connects this inward turn of American writers with what James, in his *Varieties,* calls that "enormous sense of inner authority and illumination" that comes from the "revelations" of possible worlds, worlds consciously realized but thwarted by the outward environment. The "voice" within claims its authority, in other words, against those outside itself as it impels the writer to build its world. Poirier significantly underscores the extent that Twain's characters submit to this commanding urge as he alters his perspective in chapter 15.

Our interpretations part ways over the success of this focal shift. From chapter 15 on, Poirier claims that Twain's attempts to free Huck within his hero's own mental recesses fail through the author's inability to express such a liberating transformation. Without the language necessary for integrating its hero's thinking within a larger scheme of relations, Twain's novel "discovers that the consciousness it values most cannot expand within the environment it provides, that the self cannot come to fuller life through social drama."[17] I maintain, however, that it is precisely the particular set of social relations themselves that sets the stage for the liberating moves Twain dramatizes within his hero's consciousness. And as we re-connect Twain's exploration of his hero's mind to the vocabulary of James, we can return to the interplay of pungent terms within Huck's consciousness and within the

16. Richard Poirier, *A World Elsewhere: The Place of Style in American Literature,* 188.
17. Ibid., 193–95.

relations therein that crystallize our sense of the nature of Jim's reality.

With this notion of a verbal interplay, we can extend James's theory of relations beyond the intimate interests of the ego into the ego's more complex set of epistemological relations, within what James called the "stream of thought, of consciousness, or of subjective life." Within this mental stream, "consciousness does not appear to itself chopped up in bits," as James explained; rather "it flows"; within his metaphor James attempted to capture the mind operating in what he saw as its natural state (*Psychology*, 1:239). Likewise, Twain leads us into the flow of Huck's thoughts, as the idea of Jim slips into his hero's mental stream even as Jim himself slips into the river. Yet the idea enters into the middle of the plenitude of continuous thoughts that James described as a "community of self," a self inclusive of all former tributaries of thought (*Psychology*, 1:239). Although we may consider Jim's piercing use of "frens" as predicating the nature of his reality within Huck's mind, that reality is still open to doubt as it relates with former ideas of Jim meandering through Huck's mental stream. These include the images of Jim as nigger, Jim as slave, and Jim as the Widow's property, which, in Huck's mind, intermingle with the new image of Jim as friend.

To allow this other idea a solid place in Huck's "community of self" will mean altering or expanding that self. As he depicts Huck slowly transforming and determining his own world of "living realities," Twain offers a parallel to James's reality theory in firmly linking Huck's ego to his developing idea of Jim. This self-creative process, however, brings us back to the complete flow of relational thought and James's central metaphor, the stream of consciousness. For "*whatever* the content of the Ego may be," as it anchors our realities, "it must form a *liaison*," as James emphasized, "between all the things of which we become successively aware" (*Psychology*, 1:242). The construction of reality, then, moves out from the center of the self and not in upon it; for now James's use of ego may suffice for that nuclear point of identity, and thus the self can be seen as redistributing its boundaries beneath its own power.[18] However, before that power—

18. One of James's more colorful definitions of the ego can be found in his analogy of the herdsman. "The herd's unity is only potential," "its centre ideal" is like a gravitational center, "until the herdsman or owner comes." The herdsman "furnishes a real centre of accretion to which the beasts are driven and by which they are held" (*Psychology*, 1:337–38).

which will definitively emerge in the form of an active will—can
assert itself within the mentations of Twain's hero, Huck must con-
ceptually link his developing image of Jim and reconcile its reality
within his own.

Again we return to the sting of Jim's voice; his words continue to
interact with Huck's stream of thought as Huck negotiates experience
into reality. In Jamesian fashion, Twain descriptively mediates
between the claims of materialism and transcendentalism. Reality is
neither purely of the mind nor merely in the world; it emerges
through the senses against actual existing data. As we move beyond
the initial prick of Jim's words, we can begin to see how word and
idea mesh within this experiential transaction. Jim's passionate
remarks, in response to Huck's thoughtless manipulation of Jim's
mind and emotions, begin to open the substantial locks upon Huck's
mental stream:

> When I got all wore out wid work, en wid de callin' for you, en
> went to sleep, my heart wuz mos' broke bekase you wuz los',
> en I didn' k'yer no mo' what become er me en de raf'. En when
> I wake up en fine you back agin, all safe en soun', de tears come
> en I could a got down on my knees en kiss' yo' foot I's so thank-
> ful. En all you wuz thinkin' bout wuz how you could make a fool
> uv ole Jim wid a lie. Dat truck dah is *trash*; en trash is what peo-
> ple is dat puts dirt on de head er dey fren's en makes 'em
> ashamed. (105)

In this passage, Jim's conjunction "en" clearly claims an ordinating
precedence. Although Twain is surely expressing Jim's emotional
state and following his sense of the demands of vernacular realism,
his conjunctive emphasis at the same time points to the more complex relations between word and thought occurring within the consciousness of Huck.

Jim's words also lead us as readers into a more intimate relation
with our own thought and language. Here it is important to note that
Jim's "dialect" is not an unmediated transcription of anyone's actual
dialect, but an elaborate literary fiction carefully constructed by
Twain. With such an artful configuration of words, Twain raises the
consciousness of his readers as he induces them to create an order
that accords with a recognizable syntax capable of making and bearing meaning. Jim's fictional dialect, in other words, commands our

attention as our senses attempt to adjust to odd sounds and appearances. Recognizable words mesh with oddly constructed ones to enhance our role as readers; we are ushered into a conscious awareness of words themselves as we search for signposts within a complex mixture of the familiar and the strange. However, like James's stream of thought, the passage as a whole flows in spite of its "chopped up" appearance; the repetitive use of initial consonant sounds, particularly the reoccurring "w" sound, helps create a sense of smoothness. In this sense, the passage provides a readerly image of the mind at work.[19]

Within James's stream of thought, human speech registers both its transitional and substantive parts through a multiplicity of such effectual relations. "There is not a conjunction or a preposition, and hardly an adverbial phrase, syntactic form, or inflection of voice," as James notes, "that does not express some shading or other of relation which we at some moment actually feel to exist between the larger objects of our thought" (*Psychology*, 1:245). Although "no existing language is capable of doing justice to all [the] shades" of multiple relations simultaneously reacting with any given idea, "the failure to register them" at all, James insists, would be the "great blunder" of any introspective analysis. "We ought to say a feeling of and, a feeling of if, a feeling of but, and a feeling of by as readily as we say a feeling of blue or a feeling of cold," as James explains, yet "language," he recognizes, "almost refuses to lend itself" to this use (*Psychology*, 1:244, 245–46). The important qualifier here is "almost."

As we continue to view chapter 15 and its concluding passage as the place where the novel focuses inward on Huck's consciousness, we can further interpret the copious use of "ands" as Twain's attempt at suggesting their effect within the stream of thought while, at the same time, implicating their epistemological role in that thought. The "ands" liberate Huck's knowledge of Jim, perforating lines of permanent thought, and the feeling of "and," like an "if" or "but," ushers substantive "thought" back into its gerundive state of "thinking." Thinking itself may be little more than a response to provocative

---

19. In *No. 44, The Mysterious Stranger*, Twain similarly raises the consciousness of his readers by presenting a rather lengthy passage in reverse; in *Joan of Arc*, he does the same as he casts its telling between fact and fiction, destabilizing authoritative language and thereby returning such authority to his readers.

transitional feelings that leave the self (or thought) in a state of disarray or with a sense of loss; as each "and," "if," or "but" inwardly registers its force, our thinking shifts, re-collects, and reconnects the self within yet another substantive thought. Thought, the self, and reality, then, if we accept James's conditions and Twain's portrayal, are not only in process but can be felt and realized as being so. This is what "we ought to say," then, as James prescribes; and this is what Twain does say through his continuing depiction of Huck's stream of thought.

Working through his transitional "ands," Twain's additive style surrounds and imbues the term "frens" with a conflux of definitions. It implies plenitude, motion, and a corresponding interior linkage within Huck's mind. Friends worry about the welfare of one another, sacrifice their time and effort to insure one another's well-being, compassionately give of themselves, and, to some degree, risk losing the self in the other. Within this relational complex, where word and idea commingle, Huck's thoughts move through and toward a more comprehensive idea of Jim. However, Huck's new apprehension still awaits internal confirmation as his consciousness streams toward fruition: a deliberate choice to act upon inner urgings through an extraordinary display of creative power. Huck has yet to perceive that without a doubt Jim's existence is as real as his own.

This is not the usual interpretation of developing relations between Jim and Huck. James L. Johnson argues, for instance, that the narrative peaks with Huck's apology to a "nigger" in the concluding scene of chapter 15. In this scene, Huck's recognition of Jim's humanity reveals a deeper acknowledgment of his reality as other; Huck sees Jim as a human being existing independently and not merely as a "subservient extension" of the self "lost in Huck's capacious ego."[20] Similarly, William Gibson points to the centrality of the same scene, but maintains that it represents the high point of the relationship between Jim and Huck, the point at which they come nearest to sealing the mutual bond of love and respect. Even Poirier, while recognizing the scene's pivotal importance for Twain's introspective analysis, suggests that following this critical juncture, Huck's consciousness develops apart from, rather than together with, its contin-

20. James L. Johnson, *Mark Twain and the Limits of Power: Emerson's God in Ruins*, 96–97.

uing external relations. For Poirier, the novel becomes a "kind of documentation of why the consciousness of the hero cannot" expand
against the relations impinging upon it.[21] However, I suggest that it
is against these very relations that Huck continues to extend the
boundaries of the self and his realization of Jim's as well. Jim, moreover, is only beginning to attach himself to the interests of Huck's
ego, outside of which he means little to the boy, but in and through
which he will come to accrue a meaning equal to, if not greater than,
that of Huck's own self. And although the relationship comes to rest
upon a significant plateau as Huck apologizes for his demeaning
trickery, it only peaks when Huck moves beyond recognizing Jim as
friend. It is a somewhat comforting plateau after all, but it calls for a
responsible act of friendship that will require Huck to renounce the
self even as he paradoxically empowers it.

James explains that such meaningful plateaus of thought are like
"resting-places" within the stream of consciousness, the "substantive
parts" of the stream that offer transitional flights of thinking, the "transitive parts," the comfort of a satisfying if provisional conclusion.
Conclusions and the desire for them, or meaning and the need to
make it, function to maintain the mental flow as James acknowledges
in his artful picture of the "wonderful stream of consciousness":

> Like a bird's life, it seems to be made of an alternation of flights
> and perchings. The rhythm of language expresses this, where
> every thought is expressed in a sentence, and every sentence
> closed by a period. The resting-places are usually occupied by
> sensorial imaginations of some sort . . . contemplated without
> changing; the places of flight are filled with the thoughts of rela-
> tions, static or dynamic, that for the most part obtain between the
> matters contemplated in the periods of rest. (*Psychology,* 1:243)

To a large degree then, meaning is established on the wing or in the
transitive parts of thought's stream, or across the span of attention
from one thought to another, while the substantive places of rest provide just that—a rest from thinking or, at least, a provisional closure
upon a significant cluster of relations.

How significant? The "important thing about a train of thought is

21. William M. Gibson, *The Art of Mark Twain,* 105–15, and Poirier, *A World
Elsewhere,* 189, 195.

its conclusion," James answers, a "word or phrase or particular image, or practical attitude or resolve," that may be "accidentally stumbled" upon or arise of itself to "fill a pre-existing gap" (*Psychology,* 1:260). A "gap" does exist within Huck's consciousness, to be filled only by Huck as the impinging presence of Jim leads him toward his own climactic resolution.

Deterministic Claims and the Sting of Training: "He's White"

To ignore these provisional meanings would be to dismiss the responsibility to act on them. Neither Twain nor James would do this. Twain would not let his protagonist do so, either. In chapter 16, Huck finds a temporary relief from his thoughts as he leaves Jim for his adventure with the raftsmen, but by chapter's end, he finds himself groping for rest again after feeling the sharp thrust of yet another of Jim's stinging words: "freedom."

"Jim said it made him all over trembly and feverish to be so close to freedom," and Huck feels just as "trembly and feverish" upon hearing Jim's words; Huck blames himself for his part in making Jim's freedom possible. "I couldn't get that out of my conscience," Huck anxiously explains, "no how nor no way. It got to troubling me so I couldn't rest; I couldn't stay in one place. It hadn't ever come home to me before, what this thing was that I was doing. But now it did; and it staid with me, and scorched me more and more" (123–24). Huck's "conscience" here might very well be explained in the same manner Jim had explained the wise decisions of Solomon, as the product of training. Huck's thought has been partially rearranged in his flight from "home," and now he attempts to find rest by falling back upon earlier comforting conclusions. In addition, Twain's use of "scorched" foreshadows one of Huck's most substantial mental images, the fires of hell reserved for those who aid and abet runaway slaves. The image stays with him as a painful reminder of guilt, revealing that it is indeed securely fastened to the deep inner reaches of his mind.

Generally, Twain's formal shift into the subject of Huck's conscience has been read as a response to such guilt. Cummings makes one of the more convincing arguments along these lines by claiming that at the "philosophical level" Twain's novel is about "everybody's enslavement to a barrage of deterministic forces"; it represents the author's "attempt to discover the cause" of their tyrannical effect "in history and human nature."[22] *Huckleberry Finn,* to expand on Cummings's insight, is about everybody's need to work through those forces to satisfying conclusions. At least this appears to be a large part of the message underlying Huck's continuing interior struggle, one that reflects and seeks to extend the domain of his love of comfort.

Training undoubtedly plays a large part in determining psychological needs; however, satisfaction relies primarily on how one negotiates particular feelings of relations, if one negotiates them at all. Making the effort to think through these multiple strands of thought may be difficult, if not painful, given the complex of interactions awaiting the attempt. As James pointed out, no idea or image exists alone within thought's stream but is "steeped and dyed in the free water" flowing around it. A "halo or penumbra" of felt relations, both "near and remote," as James continued his description, "surrounds and escorts" the image within the stream along with the "dying echo of whence it came to us" and the "dawning sense of whither it is to lead." For James, the significant worth of the image relies on the intrapsychic union of sense and matter, which, though leaving an image to be the "same *thing* it was before," nonetheless makes "it an image . . . newly taken and freshly understood" (*Psychology,* 1:255). Such a plenitude of thought may be overwhelming, carrying both traces of the past and promises for the future along with it. The experience of the whole may be overpowering to one's sense of self, and Huck cannot fully grasp its implications. This explanation partly accounts for Twain's depiction of Huck's resistance to a complete acceptance of Jim; such a depiction would substantiate the "newly taken" other but threaten, at the same time, to negate the tenaciously held known. In other words, Huck struggles to remain psychically apart from Jim even as his psyche is being drawn into an intimate union with him.

In order to accept the other fully—all that is not of the self—Huck must limit his own liberty, the liberty that he had gone to extraordinary means to acquire, including the staging of his own death. He was able to indulge the whims of the self by dying to the world. However, here was Jim, threatening to imprison the self again by imposing his reality upon Huck's own. Huck attempts to escape this

22. Cummings, *Mark Twain and Science,* 144.

compelling presence and even the thought of it by leaving Jim for his private adventure with the raftsmen. On his return, however, Huck is thrust back into his stream of thought by Jim's voicing of freedom and back into that associative activity of mind and rush of felt relations that may promise a liberating wholeness but which, for Huck, parcels out identity.

No sooner has Huck arrived back on the raft from his private experience with the raftsmen than he finds himself swimming once again through a stream of mental activity. Jim's talk of freedom and of being a "free man" echoes against the reality of Jim's friendship, which has settled within the boy's consciousness, redefining his own reality as, among many other things, being Jim's "friend." Yet Jim's unsettling talk of freedom urges Huck toward a more painful encounter with that sense of alterity still separating him from Jim. Although Jim may be a friend, he is still a "nigger," which in Huck's mind conjures up a world of difference and a different set of defining relations.

As Jim's assertion of his freedom inwardly presses the case for his own selfhood, Huck's training, cloaked as conscience, attempts to assert its authority. Conscience insists that Huck knew Jim was "running for his freedom" and that he "could have paddled a shore" to report it. However, he had let Miss Watson's "nigger go off right under [his] eyes" without saying "one single word" (124). The single word "nigger" now sets up an interplay of relations that leave Huck inwardly writhing. "I fidgeted up and down the raft," he explains, "abusing myself to myself," a pain that Huck soothes by recalling an old maxim: "give a nigger an inch and he'll take an ell" (124). The old self seems to have resisted any newly encroaching relations as Huck pleasingly settles back upon it, deciding to do its bidding by betraying Jim.

But as Huck sets off to betray him, once again Jim's word "friend" sets the "ands," and now the "ifs" as well, into motion, inwardly juxtaposing the static and dynamic images of Jim that are playing in Huck's mind:

> Pooty soon I'll be a-shoutin for joy, en I'll say, it's all on accounts o' Huck; I's a free man, en I couldn't ever ben free if it hadn' ben for Huck; Huck done it. Jim won't ever forgit you, Huck; you's de bes' fren' Jim's ever had; en you's de *only* fren' ole Jim's got now. (125)

Taking all the "tuck out of him," Jim's remarks rearrange Huck perceptually all over again, as Huck's view of his own reality now clouds over with shades of doubt. Paddling away slowly now, he "warn't right down certain" how to act (125).

How Huck is to act, however, seems less problematic to Twain than are the consequences of Huck's action. Indeed, Huck does act, confirming Jim as a free man in the encounter with the slave hunters immediately after Jim's declaration of freedom. Huck's "He's white," given to the hunter's inquiry about the color of the other man aboard the raft, brings his thinking, borrowing James's phrase, to a provisional resting place.

The experience, though, has only brought tentative relief to a Huck in transition; as the hunters leave, Huck decides to forgo any further thought about his relations with Jim, or with himself, his society and training, or the morality of his actions, or the difference between black and white. "I reckoned I wouldn't bother no more about it," Huck concludes, "but after this always do whichever come handiest at the time" (128). Twain, likewise, seems willing to forgo any further thought as he chooses the "handiest" way out of the implications of Huck's actions. Huck's declaration of Jim's whiteness has called into question the boy's own identity, going beyond its internal re-visioning to a dismantling of the differences which, in a large part, define his sense of self. If Huck is to assert his will freely, an important act that defines Twain's purpose, Huck will need to maintain some sense of self from which to act and to which he can return.

Heroism, after all, requires distinction and springs from difference. Maintaining the self's integrity is crucial if Huck's liberating efforts are to be seen as heroic. When he is in danger of losing his hero, Twain chooses to separate Jim and Huck, "smashing straight through the raft" with a steamboat resembling the jaws of hell. This time, however, Huck scrambles away from hell. At the same time, Twain scrambles away from the interactions of Huck and Jim and, for the moment, skirts the issue of free will entirely. Not long after this, Twain put the novel aside for three years—between 1876 and 1879—allowing his hero to forgo further deliberations aboard the raft, landing him instead within the mindless feuding on shore.

Until recently, critical opinion held that Twain finished his first stint of composition after completing chapter 16 and the scene in which the raft is torn apart. With the finding of the newly discovered

Huckleberry Finn manuscript, however, we now know that Twain temporarily set the work aside after a few pages into chapter 18. What matters most here is that soon after portraying the destruction of the raft and separation of Jim and Huck, Twain avoided working on the manuscript and would not return to his hero's inward deliberations and struggle toward independent being until 1883 and his third stint of composition. Not that Twain's creativity came to a halt during this period; in fact, he was busy with works such as *The Prince and the Pauper* and *Life on the Mississippi* as well as other various essays. He grew despondent, however, much as James had years earlier when reflecting on the nature of the human condition. Perplexed, Twain chose to move the question of the essential condition of humanity, whether it be free or determined, to the back of his mind—for a while.[23]

I believe that this mental distancing indicates the psychological and philosophical problems emerging within Twain's attempt to understand and portray the self within its own evolving stream, a self that was breaking down and dissolving within relations only half-realized and vaguely known. Twain may have grown despondent. On the other hand, perhaps the move away from his hero's inward drama indicates Twain's inability to articulate what James believed we could only feel within the movement of the mental stream. Such "feelings of relation" or "psychic overtones, halos, suffusions, or fringes" precede through consciousness along with our "substantive conclusions," infusing our thought with a "sensible continuity and unity" and surrounding it "like an horizon" spreading "about its meaning" (*Psychology,* 1:269–76).

Meaning is made within this horizon of experience, and the self is felt to be making it. It is here that James's notion of intimate relations connects with Twain's treatment of the same. Twain seems reluctant to compromise his hero's independence; as the feelings of relation, both inward and outward, suffuse the bond between Huck and Jim, the same "fringe" begins to diffuse Huck's identity. Simply put, the relational feelings work to pull Huck into a loving union with Jim. Although Huck's earlier apology to Jim recognized the reality of his

---

23. I would like to thank Victor Fischer of the Mark Twain Project for sending me a copy of the relevant portions of the "lost" manuscript.

otherness, his recognition still allowed him to maintain a discrete reality apart from him.

Maintaining a sense of that separateness as both necessary and credible is a large part of the novel's condition for significant freedom. As Huck drifts between the slave hunters and Jim, "the dying echo of whence [he] came," to borrow James's words, and "the dawning sense of whither" he might go, his declaration of Jim's whiteness can be seen as both a diminution and an expansion of the self, an implied dialectic that became increasingly important for Twain's later literary figures for the empowerment of the will. At this point in the novel, in other words, Huck is both willing his own being into meaning and witnessing his meaning being shaped apart from his will. Little wonder that Twain halted within this philosophical quagmire, at least for a few years until he was able to find firmer theoretical footing.

The way the conclusion of chapter 16 dovetails back to the incidents of the previous chapter suggests yet another possibility for Twain's authorial truancy. Just as Huck had resisted giving himself up to the power of the river and the whiteness of the fog, Twain's hero now resists losing himself to the implications of Jim's "whiteness" and to the powerful currents of love threatening to diffuse his sense of self. He struggles to remain apart from Jim even while becoming a part of him. Twain recognizes Jim's otherness, which allows Huck a sense of apartness, but he also recognizes that a union, by definition, dissolves the self into the whole. As Ihab Hassan explains in his study of the self in American literature, "neither the concept of difference nor the sense of alterity can wholly diffuse or empty the self," a "task [that] may devolve only upon love, ecstasy," or "mystical union."[24] Having only recently taken control of himself by symbolically feigning his own death, Huck's desire to extend his new-fashioned freedom conflicts with the equally compelling desire for love.

Some experience of controlling his own fate will finally define freedom for Huck. Yet he seems to have learned little from his liminal experience within the fog, his experience of or at the limen or threshold of consciousness, where we saw him give control of his raft to the river and control of himself to his dreams. For both Twain and

24. Ihab Hassan, *Selves at Risk: Patterns of Quest in Contemporary American Letters,* 41.

James, the limen would primarily come to represent a doorway to a wider, superior range of thought, to a higher self, as James suggested in his *Varieties;* but for now, though, Twain's description of Huck's experience on this mental frontier only points to his later depictions of more mystical dimensions of mind in *No. 44.*[25] Implied in Huck's liminal experience here, and prefiguring Twain's later more complex images, is the idea that the self is never entirely lost even when suspended within its host of relations. As Hassan similarly describes the "dissolution of self in dreams," the experience is "always dialectic, a process of loss and recovery," one that can unite the seeker and adventurer in an inward search.[26] Huck's experience in the fog and with the slave hunters, both leading into a closer union with Jim, can be read as enacting this interior dialectic, each adventure requiring Huck to recover from a parting of the self. The re-collection of his hero becomes increasingly difficult for Twain as he continues to carry Huck along toward a radical, self-assertive leap into freedom, one that he will make alone, within his thoughts.

Yet it is precisely when he is alone with his thoughts that Huck realizes most that he is not alone. Within his inmost nature, he appears divided. He continues turning inward, the self against the self, as conscience arises as a force within, bent on directing his thought's stream. Huck becomes painfully aware of the metaphorical commonplace that we can indeed be of two minds. It is more than a metaphor for Twain, however; conscience can claim a life of its own, a separate entity dividing and disabling that stream of relations James called the self. And before examining Huck's momentous encounter with this other, we need to consider Twain's concept of the divided self, one held and developed throughout his life in one form or another.

In 1876, the same year in which Twain found himself unable to continue with *Huckleberry Finn,* he read a paper before the Hartford Monday Evening Club that would eventually be published as "The Facts Concerning the Recent Carnival of Crime in Connecticut."

25. See especially James's final chapter in *Varieties* and Twain's depiction of the different levels of self in the final chapters of *No. 44.*

26. Hassan, *Selves at Risk,* 43. "Life works in wholes," as Hassan puts it, "though seemingly riddled with holes" (42). Though Twain would not have accepted the truth of this clever remark while writing his *Huckleberry Finn,* his later work begins to realize the statement.

Recalling the essay in a notebook entry for 1897, Twain wrote that it was "an attempt to account for our seeming *duality*—the presence of another *person* . . . free and independent, and with a character distinctly its own."[27] In the "Carnival of Crime," Twain struggles with this other person, a "shriveled, shabby" and "vile" dwarf, for his own freedom, which he wins after tearing his embodied conscience into "shreds and fragments" and casting the "bleeding rubbish into the fire."[28] The battle is won. Likewise, Twain's Huck would claim the victory in his own narrative, which Twain would describe as "a book of mine where a sound heart and a deformed conscience come into collision and conscience suffers defeat."[29]

But as Twain wrote in the same 1897 notebook entry, he believed that Robert Louis Stevenson had nearly caught his latest concept of the divided self in *Dr. Jekyll and Mr. Hyde*. In allowing his two distinct personages to know one another, however, he thought Stevenson had missed the mark. "Stevenson was wrong," Twain bluntly said, "for the two persons in a man are wholly unknown to each other, and can never in this world communicate with each other in any way."[30] Twain, however, would revise his concept of the divided self more than once, and having dropped the idea of an embodied conscience for the portrayal of an inward dialogue of selves in *Huckleberry Finn,* he was now moving toward a more complex theory of duality. That is, by 1897, Twain was ready to depict the dialectic of the self through the aid of yet another self, a mysterious stranger not of this world.

Responding to recent investigations into the subconscious, Twain still held that two distinct persons exist within one body but as strangers to one another. Conscience was "a part of *me,*" Twain concluded, "a creature of *training*" with "no originality" or "independence." Yet before we read this as implying that either of the two

27. Twain, *Notebook,* 348.
28. Mark Twain, "The Facts Concerning the Recent Carnival of Crime in Connecticut," 645.
29. Taken from Twain's notebook entry. Notebook no. 35 (1895), Typescript, p. 35, Mark Twain Papers, Bancroft Library, University of California, Berkeley. For a provocative discussion of "The Recent Carnival of Crime in Connecticut" and Twain's ambivalent views on the nature of conscience, especially in its relation to the ego and its solipsistic pursuits, see Gregg Camfield's *Sentimental Twain.*
30. Twain, *Notebook,* 348–49.

persons is free to function originally, we must note Twain's further complication: he added a "spiritualized self" to "this arrangement," one "dimly" perceived as being the only free agent within the whole. "I know that it and I are one," he observed; while trying to explain the "spiritual self," he noted that it lives only in dreams, "for want of a truthfuller name."[31] Mirroring his psychology, Twain's deterministic philosophy would similarly, though paradoxically, lead him to a concept of a tripartite self, one conceivably spiritual in part and therefore free from material influence.

Twain would always question the degree of freedom that might be claimed for any one action and never entirely dismissed the possibility of individual choice. However, he always qualified that choice through his particular brand of philosophy, one similar to that first typified by James as "soft determinism."[32] Though now called "compatibilism" or "complementarity," the argument remains the same: beliefs in both determinism and human freedom can be held simultaneously (probably because they must be). This, however, requires believing that freedom only means "acting without external constraint" or just "acting rightly," as James explained, and denying the "loose play" of the world necessary for effective action in it. For James, we choose "actualities" in this world that "seem to float in a wider sea of possibilities," and not conversely.[33] Twain's poetic attempts at describing this creative play of self and world, though arguably within the currents of James's own pragmatic desires, were only tentatively beginning to surface in *Huckleberry Finn*. Like his hero's quest for freedom, Twain's attempts involved struggling through the snags of a soft determinism, negating the ultimate assertion of personal independence.

The struggle would be long and drawn out through the pages of his major works, though his philosophy would find its most succinct expression in "What Is Man?," the "gospel" he began writing in 1898. Although the work was not published until 1906, and then only privately, the deterministic philosophy condensed in "What Is Man?" primarily restates the beliefs that Twain had been revising since early in his career. His complex and often confusing determinism distin-

31. Ibid.
32. William James, "The Will to Believe," in *The Will to Believe, and Other Essays in Popular Philosophy*, 149–51.
33. Ibid.

guishes between "free will" and "free choice," the first implying "untrammeled power to act as you please," and the second "but a mere *mental process*," the "critical ability" to determine right and wrong.[34] Twain's "mere" seems ironic here because determining one's thought may be tantamount to determining action.

Then again, it may not. "The mind can freely select, choose, point out the right and just action," according to Twain, but, unable to coerce action outside itself, "its function stops there."[35] But where is "there"? For Twain, it is back within the authoritative grip of cultural and environmental determinism, compounded by even more compelling biological influences. "Temperament and training will decide what we shall do," even though the mind is free to choose what it will think. Separating mind from body and intellect from effectual action, Twain further complicates his philosophy, like his psychology, by allowing for the possibility that a self, a "me" or "soul," exists independently of either mind or body, an elusive entity whose mystery defies definition.[36] Twain would sort through this ontological tangle more directly in his later works, but this sense of a dissociative psyche receives its early articulation in the inward drama to which we now return. Twain's fictional theorizing upon the divided self and Huck's stream of relations have only provisionally come to rest.

Thinking Toward an Independent Self: "All Right, then, I'll Go to Hell"

Henry Nash Smith reads the dramatic separation of Huck and Jim in the concluding scene of chapter 16 as the end of their quest for freedom. Any liberating thoughts that may have emerged aboard the raft are soon to be negated by the reality of shore life, according to Smith, and the life of Huck soon altered to fit the social standards once again. Poirier also considers chapter 16 to be the point at which the novel discloses that the free thinking it recommends cannot exist within the environment it has created. The rest of Huck's journey and his final struggle with his conscience is effectually meaningless, however, only if we allow the conclusion of chapter 16 to finish the strug-

34. Mark Twain, "What Is Man?," 200.
35. Ibid.
36. Ibid., 200–205.

gle as well.[37] However, by reading the second struggle as developing from and beyond the conclusion of the first, we can continue to extrapolate the implicit theorizing that links Twain to James in their efforts to understand the nature of the stream of thought. Twain more fully describes his concept of the divided self in chapter 31, as he sets Huck's will in opposition to a now much stronger conscience, one threatening to dam ("damn") the entire stream of thought. Huck's freedom is as much, if not more, the issue here as Jim's, and his fateful choice of hell for love of Jim argues for freedom's own importance. At the same time, Twain intensifies Huck's role as thinker and, more so than previously, draws us into Huck's reflective process. Twain also leads us toward, to borrow James's words, "the place from which appear to emanate the fiats of the will" (*Psychology*, 1:298). In doing so, Twain lifts Huck beyond the actual and into the realm of the ideal.

Huck's increasing power of thinking gives ground to his bouts with conscience. Whereas his previous reflections were evoked immediately upon social interaction, in response to the stinging terms that bored their way into consciousness and set thoughts moving through a stream of relations, Huck now purposely engages his mind after hearing that Jim had been sold back into slavery. "I went to the raft, and set down in the wigwam to think," he says; "I thought, till I wore my head sore" (268). He thinks on, however, about leaving Jim to his fate and about himself if he were to attempt to alter that fate. But "conscience went on grinding" him to think that even his thinking about Jim reveals his own hypocrisy, which brings forth thoughts of "Providence" and his own fate. Then thinking about praying, he nearly gives it up until, writing the lie, he finds it impossible to pray. He will betray Jim. But Huck "set there thinking" a little while longer about his letter of resolve, thinking how he had barely saved himself from eternal damnation. "And went on thinking. And got to thinking" of his true relation to Jim (268–70).

Within this interior dialogic conflict these relations begin to play their part, as Twain reveals the self in the making, or the self within its own determining power. Depicting James's claim that "the whole

37. Henry Nash Smith, *Mark Twain: The Development of a Writer*, 116–17, and Poirier, *A World Elsewhere*, 195, 202.

drama is a mental drama," Twain sets Jim upon the center stage of Huck's mind:

> And I see Jim before me . . . and we a floating along, talking, and singing, and laughing. . . . I'd see him standing my watch on top of his'n . . . so I could go on sleeping, and see him how glad he was when I come back out of the fog . . . [He] would always call me honey, and pet me, and do everything he could think of for me, and how good he always was . . . and said I was the best friend old Jim ever had in the world, and the *only* one he's got now. . . . (270)

Huck has been here before, Jim's earlier talk of freedom scorching his conscience, and much the same cast continues to play within the inner drama. Twain now depicts Huck's recollections, however, more harmoniously, with little violation of grammatical and syntactical form, suggesting that when given the time to reflect, the mind orders its own language in its own image.

Such an interpretive suggestion again solicits the reader's co-creative labor. Pausing and thinking, Huck orders and clarifies the significant bearings of his own thought; in so doing he begins to believe in his thought as fact. In Jamesian terms, Huck struggles to bring his thoughts to rest upon his own substantial meanings. Only then, upon the firm footing of his convictions, can Huck truly experience freedom in action. When given "live champions," as James puts it in *Pragmatism,* such beliefs "become actual things." Thinking through an experience, then, in this case the imposition of word and image, may open a "gap that we can spring into," as James further suggests. This gap, in effect, evokes our own creative act (128–29). James's own words appear to be a concerted attempt to fashion our roles not only as readers but also as thinkers:

> Our acts, our turning-places, where we seem to ourselves to make ourselves, and grow, are the parts of the world to which we are closest, the parts of which our knowledge is the most intimate and complete. Why should we not take them at their face-value? Why may they not be the actual turning-places and growing-places which they seem to be, of the world—why not the workshop of being, where we catch fact in the making, so that nowhere may the world grow in any other kind of way than this? (129)

Like Twain's textual provocations, which usher his readers into a similar "workshop of being," James's pragmatism demands an individual and creative response to experience.

Huck, however, has not yet found the inner strength to leap forward into his own creative gap. In fact, Twain's use of the pronoun "I" seems markedly pronounced in this passage as Huck recalls the presence of Jim; the emphasis suggests that Huck is nearly losing himself in his own reflections as he sits absorbed in the flights of his thinking. Twain, however, has not carried his hero into yet another tug of relations only to have him relinquish himself to the most dominating character, whether it be his idea of Jim, his egoistic "I," or the composite force of his training. It is time for another Huck to take center stage or for that "central nucleus" of the self, as James defines it, "the source of effort and attention," to determine its own action (*Psychology,* 1:297–98). Although Twain may not entirely accept the reality of such a self because his lingering determinism denied its certain existence, he nonetheless risks positing it at least as an ideal. For Huck, this is the place from which he will draw the necessary self-determining strength.

In *Psychology* and its chapter "The Consciousness of Self," James defines this ideal part of personal consciousness, where our will, thought, conscience, and moral sense all coalesce, as the "spiritual self," that "intimate part of the self" felt as and within the thinking process (1:296). Although he concretely defines the spiritual self as a part of thought's stream, he understands how, in an "abstract way," it may be divided into its faculties such as the will and conscience, "isolating them" within a "plurality" of identities in order to understand the whole (1:296). However, whether the spiritual self is divided or integrated, "our considering [it] at all is a reflective process," as James explains, one which enables us "to think of ourselves as thinkers" and to know our thinking as peculiarly our own (1:296).

Revealing his own tendency to divide the concept of the self, a tendency toward dualism with which James continues to struggle even as he denies it for psychological purposes, James considers the stream of personal consciousness abstractly in order to defend the phenomenal self:

> If the stream as a whole is identified with the Self far more that any outward thing, a certain portion of the stream abstracted

from the rest is so identified in an altogether peculiar degree, *and is felt* . . . as a sort of innermost centre within the circle, of sanctuary within the citadel, constituted by the subjective life as a whole. (1:297)

The important phrase here is *"and is felt,"* as James emphasizes, and whether we call it ego, soul, or self, this central part of consciousness is "no *mere ens rationis,* cognized only in an intellectual way, and no *mere* summation of memories or *mere* sound of a word in our ears" (1:299). Instead, when engaged, the spiritual self is sensed directly within its stream of relations as thinking wrestles its way toward doing.

No more apt image of James's spiritual self could be found than that of Huck sitting and thinking alone within the wigwam aboard the raft as the entire structure drifts downstream on the Mississippi River. Within this floating citadel, Huck sits down to think and in thinking finds that peculiar presence of mind James describes as the core of being, the phenomenally known self. Twain's description of his hero's experience within this inner sanctum enlivens James's speculations as Huck's feelings and cognitions intertwine within what James calls the "palpitating inward life" (*Psychology,* 1:299). Not only does Huck's head ache from thinking about Jim's predicament but his heart does as well.

Huck's thinking begins to sting in much the same way that Jim's words had previously stung him into action. Impelled by his thinking, Huck's feelings career from one extreme to another. He thinks to himself, then his thoughts move out toward Jim, the King and Duke, Jim again, and back on Tom Sawyer and Miss Watson; forward to "nigger" Jim, freedom, and his own fate; then to conscience, God, and church; landing uncomfortably with his thoughts in the "everlasting fire" (268–69). Twain's use of interior dialogue certainly allows us to enter his hero's thoughts, and given the rush and extent of imagery—from Huck himself and out to God and back—within a single paragraph, Twain arguably prefigures the stream of consciousness technique of later writers.

Twain surpasses a mere display of technique, however; like James, he relates the spiritual self, the central current within the stream of being, to "some sort of junction" or psychic terminal through which "ideas or incoming sensations are 'reflected' or pass over into outward acts." The connection leaves its impression and, to reemphasize James's point, the whole experience is felt. This is the same point that Twain also makes in the passage opening with Huck's streaming thoughts. Not only does Huck feel his thoughts like blows to the head, but also, in playing his colloquial phrasings off of particularly active verbs, Twain thrusts them upon his readers, literally personifying the psychic life.

"My conscience went to grinding me," Huck tells us, as he begins feeling "low-down and ornery." His thinking keeps on grinding until he feels it slapping him, as conscience and "Providence" play off one another in his head until, trying his best to "soften" the blows within, he ends up literally shivering from thought (268–69). This is hardly one of Huck's more comfortable trips down the Mississippi, yet it begins to reveal the same "direct sensible acquaintance" that James suggests to be the phenomenal proof for a spiritual self, one singularly felt to be at the center of one's existence.

Moreover, Huck's apprehension of this psychic center begins to acquire a larger significance if we accept the terms James provides for understanding this experience. Although it is in many ways similar to Twain's, James's description in the *Psychology* differs by providing a working vocabulary, or a sharable one, as James suggested, for moving from inward thought to outward action. The awareness of this "palpitating inward life," as James put it, breaks in upon us through a "constant play of furtherances and hindrances" in our thinking, "of checks and releases, tendencies" running with "desire" and those running "the other way," some aligning "themselves on the side of thought's interests," some with its more "unfriendly part" (1:299). But who or what enters into this internal division with decisive authority? When, to use James's figurative language, does the subjective drama play upon the objective stage of the world? James's answer points only vaguely to the "what" or the "who," while Twain depicted the "when" through his hero's enactment of his will. However it is within James's pseudo-scientific reasoning (or rational spirituality) that he and Twain met on viable grounds, and this heuristic triangle can best be read within a psychology of the spiritual self that will enable them to actuate their theories.

"The mutual inconsistencies and agreements, reinforcements and obstructions, which obtain amongst [the] objective matters" within this "central active self," James explained while continuing his introspective argument, "reverberate backwards and produce what seem to be incessant reactions of my spontaneity upon them, welcoming or opposing, appropriating or disowning, striving with or against," and of primary importance, "saying yes or no" (1:299). James's choice of "my spontaneity," a phrase derived from the Latin *sponte* and meaning "of free will," goes beyond mere description to a declaration of the essential nature of the stream of thought. The stream is possessed by a "my" that freely responds to a world of actualities choosing to make one or the other possible. James's language also reveals that although he resisted dualistic schemes, he found it increasingly difficult to move linguistically beyond them. For now the "my," of necessity, must remain. And it appears to remain within the actions of the will.

For Twain this is certainly the case. Although the concept of the will as a mental faculty, a dynamic inward force of sorts, might be waning in contemporary thinking, for Twain and James it was still a viable force, and the question of its freedom was central to the problem of determinism and to their theorizing upon the stream of consciousness.

James had to resolve the issue in his own mind before he could confidently assert either his psychology or his philosophy and, as it must have seemed to him at one point, before he could even continue his life. He had to believe in free will, as he recorded in a notebook entry for 1870, in order to believe in his "individual reality and creative power." Such a belief was not blindly optimistic, as James was quick to point out, but instead was one that enables the building of a life in "doing and suffering and creating."[38] Twain could never be so certain, though he would build his own psychology, if not his life, around a similar ideal of freedom. The shaping of that ideal began with Huck Finn.

In returning to the raft intent on thinking about Jim, Huck sets in motion the ideal will that, in Jamesian terms, works out from the inwardly divisive struggle of thought. Within the same terms, Huck's maintaining of Jim's image before his mind, while other choices present themselves in an onslaught of opposing thoughts, in itself frees the will to act with or against those choices. Arriving within the node of being, to paraphrase James, Huck makes the active connection: "It

---

38. James, *Letters*, 1:148. James's son Henry adds this note to the collected letters of his father.

was a close place . . . I was a trembling, because I'd got to decide, forever, betwixt two things, and I knowed it. I studied a minute, sort of holding my breath, and then says to myself: 'All right, then, I'll *go* to hell' . . ." (270-71). The "betwixt two things" certainly complicates interpretation, especially since our own study of this critical moment— or "minute"—must now remain outside the represented mental drama.

To send or not to send the letter that would negate Jim's freedom is the immediate problem. Huck destroys the letter, but he knows— and feels—his decision to have even more import. The finality of his "forever" argues its own case here. The "forever" also leads us into a paradox. The force of Huck's training is such that he seems unable to think independently from his conditioning language and environment; yet thinking out from his conditioned self, he acts against it by willing his own fate. But could Twain posit the will's freedom even against his tendency toward philosophical determinism, his always tenuous belief in the possibility of such freedom? He could if we allow that his psychology divided the self along the same lines as his deterministic philosophy.

As we have seen, Twain's soft determinism maintains that the mind can point out the morally correct action but cannot freely enact its choice outside itself. Even if we were to think ourselves out from under the force of our training, we would still remain prisoners, as Twain explained it, of those inborn dispositions he puts under the rubric of temperament. Regardless of the freedom to which Huck's thinking leads him, then, it can lead him no further than the frontier of his own temperament. Huck's action to free Jim following his choice to do so might well argue for no more than the boy responding with a good heart.

But more might be involved. Twain's own type of soft determinism allows for the possibility of a liberated "soul," and even within the mechanical concept of human existence that dominates "What Is Man?," he leaves space for the divine within our inmost nature. Though eluding definition, Twain concedes that the "Soul" may be that part of "the Me" where the "mental *and* spiritual combine" and in an "indeterminate fashion" direct the whole of one's being. "Maybe," Twain hedges, but this "maybe" makes all the difference in the world, and all the difference to our being in the world.[39]

39. Twain, "What Is Man?," 205.

James takes up the notion of the "Soul" as well throughout his *Psychology*. In "The Consciousness of the Self" and "The Mind-Stuff Theory" chapters he specifically examines the "Soul-Theory," only to ultimately reject its traditional concept for the purposes of psychology in general. However, his own psychology, especially his theorizing on the central or spiritual self, may be read as affirming some notion of a soul. "Why on earth doesn't the poor man say the *Soul* and have done with it," James imagines his readers asking (1:180). He would if the term could be conceived outside of its dualistic implications and the "substantialist view" that defines the "Soul" as a separate entity, "something behind the present Thought, another kind of substance, existing on a non-phenomenal plane" (1:345).

James would not deny that there may be more to being human than just the coexistence of mind and body:

> It is, in fact, with the word Soul as with the word Substance in general. To say that phenomena inhere in Substance is at bottom only to record one's protest against the notion that the bare existence of the phenomena is the total truth. A phenomenon would not itself be, we insist, unless there were something *more* than the phenomenon. To the more we give the provisional name of Substance. (1:346)

As James suggests, calling the "more" the soul solves nothing; it only inhibits the understanding of ourselves as a whole and spirit as a part of, not distinct from, the phenomenal self. This self is enough for James's psychology. In one of his metaphysical digressions, he speculates upon the "more" as being "some sort of an *anima mundi* thinking in all of us," something like a collective breath of consciousness or universal stream of thought. However, as he shifts away from such proto-Jungian notions, James insists that the "phenomena are enough" for psychology, since "the passing Thought itself is the only *verifiable* thinker" and its functioning all we can hope to know (1:346-47). This worked for James, perhaps, but again Twain was not so certain in his own thinking, and not yet ready to accept the self within such Jamesian terms.

Twain also could not separate his psychology from his philosophy as James appeared able to do. Twain's philosophical determinism, by allowing for a soul at all, necessarily divides the self into one part determined and one part free. Although Twain and James developed their theories of consciousness along similar lines, this critical difference remains. If the self acts freely, then for James it is part of the nature of thought, albeit a spiritual part felt within its inmost nature; however, for Twain, free action necessitates supernatural thought and the spiritual self, though existing within, remains apart. The self is free to act in either hypothesis, but for Twain it does so out of division.

Huck's "I'll go to hell," then, still might be read as his climactic moment of self-assertion, a moment of self-empowerment. But who or what is asserting power? Or, rather, what self is willing to suffer hell for another's sake? "Maybe" the "me," that spiritual center of the mind which may be its saving grace, at least for the deterministically inclined Twain. If this be so, then Twain's psychology goes no further than his philosophy, for he represents Huck's actions as being ultimately out of Huck's control. "After all this long journey," to borrow Huck's words, "here was it all come to nothing" (268). But Twain's philosophy, oscillating between the demands of determinism and the desire for freedom, does allow that the "soul" may be a combination of the mental and spiritual, and in working this combination into his psychology through Huck's crucial reflections, Twain momentarily subverts his deterministic philosophy, freeing Huck's will.

James explained this liberating combination as leading to a peculiar shift in consciousness, one that moves us from the "indicative" to the "imperative" mood, from thinking "it *is*" to "*let it be*" (2:569). Although he further acknowledged in *Psychology* that the final force that moves us from knowing to doing remains a mystery, he nonetheless posited the actions of the will as responsible for carrying knowledge within the range of physical response. In fact, the will may compel a response, if adamantly engaged. However, the engagement and concentration of the will is freely done, according to James, though not without the effort that in itself argues for volitional freedom: the effort to retain a difficult idea within the mind against strong oppositional thinking (2:561).

James's "effort of attention" is the "essential phenomenon of the will," and, practically speaking, the will's work is done when the idea has secured its presence within our thought (2:562–64). If the new reality is tenaciously held, then the mind will consent to its existence, James believes, and will enact that reality upon the world. The religious connotations are not to be missed here, when James insists that our salvation depends on our ability to maintain the right idea unwaveringly before the mind (2:565).

Twain echoes this idea as he carries Huck to his own moment of salvation in chapter 31, to those "awful thoughts" and "awful words" of apparent damnation, words that, once spoken, release the awe-filled Huck from the hell of his training. "I shoved the whole thing out of my head," he declares as he determines to free Jim. Neither Twain nor James, however, could account for the physical action that links the spiritual to the material, the thinking to doing, though James himself acknowledged that something more is involved.

James does suggest, however, that in the case of a "healthy" will, one whose "fiat" follows upon the necessary "amount of complication" within the thinking process, the best action follows. An ideal action, in other words, follows after deliberation within the stream of one's thoughts, after working through "all the forces" there vying for one's attention along with the further relative ideas with their own impulses and consequential associations. After engaging all these forces and thinking through their urgings, James steps out on a limb by suggesting that "a vision of which course is best" immediately precedes the "fiat . . . and where the will is healthy, the vision must be right . . . and the action must obey the vision's lead" (2:536). This flash of vision seems beyond the purview of language or the descriptive powers of both Twain and James, though Twain certainly leads his hero to its threshold. Although Huck's ideal actions to liberate Jim are constrained by actual conditions, the habitual prejudices Huck knows so well, his immediate decision to risk himself for Jim argues for the health of his own will.

Still, the question of vision itself lingers. Who or what flashes such a compelling insight before the mind's eye? James as psychologist confesses to be at a loss here, although on a religious level, he suggests that the impulse springs from a compelling "still small voice" within our inmost nature. Huck's critical reflection suggests the same, although like the voices in the fog, this one seems beyond a natural explanation.

It seems that the point, just as Jim had suggested, is down deeper for Twain and James. But the point for them is not only in the way

we are raised but in the way we might ourselves partake in the raising. Both men desired an active part; reflection alone is not enough,
and it is this desire for action that, in a large part, shaped their psychology. Both men were reformers as well as thinkers. Although the
image of consciousness as a stream centers on thought in process,
thinking itself, as both Twain and James described it, evolves both
within and against itself—even against the world, if need be. Their
psychology points to a division within, a struggle for the possession
of one's field of consciousness, a field, as James wrote in his chapter
entitled "Will," won only by the "heroic mind" (*Psychology,* 2:564, 78).
Huck's thoughts and actions certainly cast him as a Jamesian hero
here.

The crucial point of *Huckleberry Finn,* then, occurs with Huck's
heroic assertion of freedom. This moment claims that we are essentially free within our thoughts, and that through these thoughts we
are potentially free in the world outside. As writer and moralist,
Twain sought to further this liberating claim, and his portrait of Joan
of Arc contributes significantly toward this goal. To develop his
notion of the divided self within his portrayal of Joan's voices, in particular, Twain leads us into a more serious consideration than Huck
Finn provides of the ongoing dialectic between impositions from
without, and the liberating thought issuing from within.

Verifying the Truth that Matters
Personal Recollections of Joan of Arc

Meanwhile we have to live today by what truth we can
get today, and be ready tomorrow to call it falsehood.
—William James, *Pragmatism*

*M*ark Twain as hagiographer seems improbable, yet this is whom we encounter when reading the *Personal Recollections of Joan of Arc*. From his opening preface through the concluding paragraphs, Twain never tires in his praise of Joan, consistently holding her forth as worthy of our imitation and even our veneration. Miracles abound in the book, and the extraordinary nearly becomes the commonplace. The mystical and magical play across a harsh political reality; the effusively emotional, sentimental, and melodramatic obfuscate the claim of historical accuracy to which the narrative evidently aspires. Through it all, Twain's Joan emerges as an image of perfectly reconciled thought and action, an exemplary marriage of human genius and divine intellect, bold in spirit, pure, good, and true. Such laudatory coloration might well be expected in the biography of a saint, but few would expect Mark Twain to engage in such a style even when recounting a saintly life— but he did.

Albert Bigelow Paine, Twain's official biographer, felt it necessary to defend *Joan of Arc* against contemporary critics who believed Twain "had gone out of his field" by writing a historical romance. "It is the ultimate of realism, too," as Paine maintained, distinguishing

Twain's style from the trend of literary naturalism ushering in the twentieth century, "not hard, sordid, or ugly realism, but noble, spiritual, divine realism."[1] Perhaps more idealistic than divine, Twain's presentation of Joan and her narrative—moralistic in tone, allusively religious, even mystical in mood, yet starkly uncomplicated in characterization—is surprising.

That might be the reason why Twain's *Joan of Arc*, for the most part, continues to be denied sustained attention by modern critics. Although Twain attempted to represent Joan as a powerful or even transcendent figure like Huck or his eventual mysterious stranger, as James L. Johnson points out, his personal devotion to his subject and faith in her history "ruined his art" by providing him with a "ready-made plot and a ready-made attitude" and even "a ready-made saint." Twain was to find no literary blueprint for constructing Joan of Arc, however, within his sources; rather he believed historical fact to be malleable and intended to participate more in its shaping than its parroting. However, most critics, like Johnson, are seemingly content to let the novel remain in "deserved obscurity."[2]

However deserved that obscurity, the fact remains that in *Joan of Arc* Twain continued to explore the problems that complicated his earlier theorizing upon consciousness in *Huckleberry Finn*. The question of whether being in reality is free or determined, or a complex mixture of the two, and the related tensions of the apparent divisions of the mind, which were deployed so dramatically in Huck's internal dialogues, are still the problems compelling Twain's attention. With *Joan of Arc*, Twain focused his attention even more sharply on that liminal kind of experience in which we found Huck drifting aimlessly through the Mississippi River fog. Twain constructed for Joan dreamlike phenomena that offer us a means for understanding her religious experiences; while we focus primarily on Twain's treatment of Joan's mysticism, we can also explore why her voices and visions are particularly central to Twain's developing theory of a divided self. *Joan of Arc* is an important link between the realistic or naturalistic investigations into consciousness as fictionalized in *Huckleberry Finn*

1. Albert Bigelow Paine, *Mark Twain: A Biography*, 3:1029, 1031. Paine would eventually write his own biography of Joan, and his devotion to both her and Twain colors his remarks here.
2. Johnson, *Mark Twain and the Limits of Power*, 159–60.

and the more metaphysical, spiritual, even supernatural theorizing about the self figured in Twain's *No. 44, The Mysterious Stranger*. In all three works Twain celebrated independent thought by developing a novelistic image of a psychology that reflects our capacity for interior kinds of significant freedom.

If Joan is Twain's exemplary model of independent thought, then her encounter with religious experience must somehow reflect her capacity for such intellectual independence; however, Joan's voices appear to think for her, or rather her own faculties seem subject to the will of her voices rather than to a will of her own. For many readers, Joan's own voice seems actually imprisoned within a layer of other voices claiming authority over her life and its import. At the same time, it is also safe to say that Twain believed her very life could nevertheless speak through the binding and blinding voices of heavenly angels and earthly politics and liberate free thought into effective action. The central problem for Twain, then, involves the possibility of liberation in the face of divine will. He must free Joan and the truth she embodies from her historical bonds and return them both to a sense of the contingency of the moment. We, as readers of our own time, will need to reshape her experiences within a conceptual frame contemporary with Twain's, one that enables a more modern appropriation of them. For that framework, we turn again to William James.

James can serve as a kind of cultural mirror in which to read Twain because James's belief in independent thought and its efficacious movement in the world became the cornerstone for his powerful pragmatism. His thinking embodied a metaphysics of freedom that enabled authentic movement of the individual toward a realization of truth within and upon the world. The words "authentic" and "truth," in fact, present a special problem when we consider any action of key interest to Twain in his portrait of Joan's ideal personality. I intend to use James's somewhat idiosyncratic theory of truth to assist in an examination of the way in which Twain deflated historical and literary authority in his effort to clear the way for fresh discourse concerning Joan's life and to find literary means for authenticating the "true" idea of freedom he found there. Although not formally set down in writing until the 1907 publication of *Pragmatism: A New Name for Some Old Ways of Thinking*, James's notions of truth and the individual's part in its realization permeated his thinking and found their way into nearly all of his major work. These notions dovetail back through his popularly acclaimed *The Varieties of Religious Experience* to his seminal *The Principles of Psychology,* providing James with a pragmatic sense of purpose.

We begin with a reading of the prefatory pages of Twain's *Joan of Arc* in the light of James's theory of truth. In the front matter of the novel, Twain indirectly takes up the problem of literary and historical truth. His fictive screening of the facts surrounding Joan's life appears to run counter to all efforts to ascertain the truth within and among the facts. I say "appears" because, through comparison with James's theory of truth, Twain's opening dislocative strategies prepare the way for his own authorization of the facts through a verification of their truth in quite modern terms. The most problematical aspects of the truth lie in the degree of authority ascribed to Joan's religious experiences. I will be using James's *Psychology* and *Varieties* in conjunction with his pragmatist notions of truth to suggest how Twain could argue the reality of her voices and visions in terms of modern experience.

All three of James's texts contribute significantly to a usable map for reading Twain's *Joan of Arc,* a work that, however problematic its style, looks to a saintly life and spiritual experience for an encounter in which the possibilities of true freedom can be divined. Both the course of such a life and a set of such experiences display the inner workings of an emergent self; Twain was attempting to authenticate the idea of truth as experiential process rather than conceptual structure. That brings us to the verification process central to James's pragmatist understanding of the nature of such truth and Twain's own affiliations with it.

Fancy Work in the Front Matter and an Unreliable Narrator

"Truth *happens* to an idea," James explained in his chapter "The Notion of Truth" in *Pragmatism*; "It *becomes* true, is *made* true by events. Its verity *is* in fact an event, a process: the process namely of its verifying itself, its veri-*fication*. Its validity is the process of its valid-*ation*" (92). James's use of "events" underscores his emphasis on experience and our own relations within the particulars of experience. The true idea is the one that works best in leading us through these particulars and on "towards other moments" of experience, or eventful verifications, "which it will be worth while to have been led to" (94). An idea authenticates its own value as truth not only by continuing the process but also by valuing the experience to which it leads.

However, what might be the meaning of a worthwhile leading? Pragmatically, it refers to the functional life of an idea in the world, as James explained, an idea that allows us to move through experiential realities, in the most expedient manner, toward the realization of useful ideals. The experiences can be either concrete occurrences or abstract ideas and principles. "Between the coercions of the sensible order and those of the ideal order, our mind is thus wedged tightly," James acknowledged, and any idea that helps us to exist advantageously between the two verifies its own truth. At the same time, that idea points to a prior verification by someone, somewhere, and at some time (*Pragmatism,* 95–96). James considered engaging in this continual process of verifying and furthering such true ideas a "primary human duty," one that calls upon us to complete the function of truth as long as it continues verifying itself within experience (*Pragmatism,* 93). Ideas cease to be true, James suggested, when entertained apart from their use; in other words, without a viable use, an idea can claim no true reality.

Like James, Twain found the validating and maintaining of true ideas a compelling "duty," and his pursuit of the facts verifying the reality of Joan of Arc led him to his own means of authenticating them. For the most part, Twain's narrative remains closely tied to historical fact, but the significance of this historical accuracy becomes clear only after a close examination of the ten pages of prefatory matter that precede the text proper.

Beginning with the title page, Twain mixes historical fact with blatant fiction, an opening strategy that, though not dismissing the historical claims upon his subject matter, frees it from the silent, hence repressive, authority of received data and allows him to build his own system for the verification of history's events. Twain's title prepares us for such shuffling of fact and fiction:

> "*Personal Recollections of Joan of Arc,* by the Sieur Louis de Conte (her page and secretary), freely translated out of the ancient French into modern English from the original unpublished man-

uscript in the National Archives of France, by Jean François Alden."[3]

His title, in its rhetorical rotundity, provides an authority that, upon closer examination, evaporates before our eyes. The title, in only a few dozen words, finally identifies the source of its authority as Jean François Alden, who is, as an authority for this book, a fiction.

To muddy the waters further, Twain's naming of this fictive authority may have been an inside joke. Henry Alden, an editor at *Harper's,* had refused to publish Twain's satire of Samuel Royston's *The Enemy Conquered, or, Love Triumphant,* because Twain had included Royston's entire novelette in his article, as a means of revealing its "literary idiocy" firsthand. "God almighty, this is editing with a gaudy intelligence," Twain wrote to Fred J. Hall in 1892, pretending to fail to understand Alden's obvious reasons for rejecting the article. Twain's use of "Alden" as translator, along with his list of examined authorities, may have been meant as a sarcastic reminder to *Harper's* that Twain could indeed distinguish his own work from that of another.

It would also seem, at first, that the "personal recollections" must be Joan's own; however, could they rather be those of de Conte? or Joan's, as remembered by de Conte? For that matter, who is de Conte? Is he truly the page that recorded Joan's recollections? Could he be the "page" upon which his own recollections are recorded? Finally, who "freely translates" what? Twain may in fact be inviting us to do so, to participate in his playful mood, since he even rewrites the name of the page (de Conte) that narrates Joan's story. If no set of "recollections" by a Sieur Louis de Conte exists as such, a set by a Louis de *Coutes* does. De Coutes was Joan's real page and his memories of her were recorded during the process of her rehabilitation in 1450. He was with her from the start of her military adventures until their end at the gates of Paris; his recollections are on file in the official records of France. Joan actually had three pages or secretaries, all of whom testified on her behalf during her posthumous "retrial" and "rehabilitation" process. Little is known about Louis de Coutes except that he was a courtly youth of no more than fourteen or fifteen when he served with Joan. Wilfred T. Jewkes provides some

3. Mark Twain, *Personal Recollections of Joan of Arc.* Subsequent references will be given parenthetically in the text.

sense of de Coute and the page's admiration for Joan in his collection of testimonies given at Joan's trial and during her rehabilitation
process. De Coute's testimony during the rehabilitation, as might
be expected, painted Joan as both a saint and a national hero. "She
was very abstemious" and often survived on little more than "a
hunk of bread," he recalls, but her strength in battle often super-
seded that of her soldiers.[4]

Twain's "de Conte" can, by the instrumental sense of the French
particle "de," signify "by means of the story" as well as echo a real
historical name; Twain may be playing with his narrator's name in an
effort to loosen his story from the single historical perspective of
de Coutes and link it more into the kind of authority we associate
with fiction. Twain's story of Joan, in fact, collates various historically
documented recollections of Joan's friends and companions. Twain
records all of this documentation through the persona of his Sieur
Louis de Conte, who, to make matters more interesting, shares his ini-
tials with Samuel Langhorne Clemens. To elaborate on Twain's word
play, Twain records his particular truth upon the "page" that he uses
to fashion Joan's story.

Strictly speaking, of course, if there were no de Conte, then no
translation of de Conte's personal narrative exists either; Twain's
inclusion of a Jean Francois Alden as translator of a nonexistent text
then completes his parody of textual authority and opens the way for
his own imaginative engagement in establishing his own authority.
However, none of the official records pertaining to the life of Joan of
Arc were available to Twain in "modern English," though they were
all available in modern French. This fact points to the second page of
Twain's front matter and its list of "authorities examined in verification of the truthfulness of this narrative." These included French and
English writers, Catholics and Protestants, poets, biographers, and
historians, all of whom built their own histories, biographies, and
romances around the historical facts and according to their own
diverse and often revisionist agendas.

Twain's list includes J. E. J. Quicherat's *Condamnation et Réhabilitation de Jeanne d'Arc*, J. Fabre's *Procès de Condamnation de*

---

4. Wilfred T. Jewkes *Joan of Arc: Fact, Legend, and Literature*, 66–67. Jewkes
also provides a few selections from the early French "chronicles" pertaining to
Joan's military accomplishments.

Jeanne d'Arc, H. A. Wallon's *Jeanne d' Arc,* M. Sepet's *Jeanne d'Arc,* J. Michelet's *Jeanne d'Arc,* de Saint-Prix's *La Famille de Jeanne d'Arc,* de Chabannes *La Vierge Lorraine,* Monseigneur Ricard's *Jeanne d'Arc la Vénérable,* Lord Gower's *Joan of Arc,* John O'Hagan's *Joan of Arc,* and Janet Tuckey's *Joan of Arc the Maid.* In his biography of him, Paine also recalls Twain mentioning Lord Ronald Gower's biography of Joan as his other primary source of information. This was a book that provided him with a critical bibliography of the nineteenth-century literary and historical treatment of Joan.[5]

Quicherat and Michelet were the most important of Twain's sources, however, for they provided modern French translations of the actual recollections of de Coutes. In his five-volume work, with the complete title *Procès de Condamnation et de Réhabilitation de Jeanne d' Arc, dite La Purcelle* (1841-1849), Quicherat included the complete text of the trial and rehabilitation process, selections from the French chronicles, letters, public documents, and even financial accounts documenting Joan's military expenses. Working from the same documents, Michelet published them in a more popular, narrative form in his monumental *History of France,* published in French in 1841 and translated into English by 1845. Michelet and Quicherat, as Twain told Albert Bigelow Paine, were two of his "chief sources of information," and he had worked laboriously to "dig" both of them out of the French.[6]

The annotations he made in his copy of Michelet's work attest to the labor that went into his translations—his command of French was less than complete—and to the importance of Michelet for his own portrait of Joan. An English translation of a section of Michelet's work, one covering the life of Joan, had been published in America by 1845, but Twain's copious annotations throughout his French copy of *Jeanne d'Arc* reveal that he attempted to work from his own translation. They also reveal that his French was good enough to carry on a critique of Michelet within his marginal comments. He could accept, for example, Michelet's confirmation that Joan never menstruated,

---

5. Thanks to Alan Gribben's *Mark Twain's Library: A Reconstruction,* we now know that Twain owned these texts and quite a few others—twenty-seven in all—concerning the life of Joan of Arc. These eleven in particular, with their interlinear markings and marginalia, point to Twain's careful and critical reading of them.

6. Paine, *Mark Twain: A Biography,* 3:958–59.

writing next to Michelet's comment on this oddity that the "higher life absorbed her & suppressed her physical development." However, he derides Michelet's chauvinistic comment that only a Frenchwoman would have been bold enough to ride with a company of men for her country's freedom, writing next to this remark "How stupid! A Joan of Arc would do it, no matter what her nationality might be. That spirit has no nationality."[7] The margins of Twain's other sources reveal this same ongoing critique of their information.

Twain had labored over Joan's history for more than a decade prior to writing her story, working through a massive bibliography, reading and annotating over twenty-five works pertaining to the saintly maid. "I have never done any work before that cost so much thinking and weighing and measuring and planning and cramming, or so much painstaking execution," Twain wrote to his friend H. H. Rogers upon finishing *Joan of Arc* in 1895, and speaking of his "authorities," he went on to explain that "no historical nugget in any of them has escaped me." In the same letter, Twain explained to Rogers that he had used "only one French history and one English one" for the first two sections of his book, "In Domremy" and "In Court and Camp," though for the final section, "Trial and Martyrdom," he "used five French sources and five English ones."[8] Twain was indeed approaching his subject matter with some care and planning.

In the book, all the major events coincide with the information gleaned from his reading, yet, as Twain further explained in his letter to Rogers, he "shoveled in as much fancy work and invention on both sides of the historical road as I pleased."[9] In the prefatory pages of *Joan of Arc,* Twain's fictive translator, J. F. Alden, says the same thing about the allegedly historical narrator de Conte. Though he cites the imaginary narrator's faithful rendition of official history as proof of his unimpeachable trustworthiness in general, he adds that de Conte's "mass of added particulars must depend for credit upon his own word alone" (ix). Not only is Twain claiming poetic license here, but in leading us back to the fictive translator, upon whom

7. See Twain's copy of *Jeanne d'Arc* in the Mark Twain Papers at Berkeley, a separate printing of the fifth volume of Michelet's seventeen-volume *Histoire de France* (Paris: Libreirie Hachette et Cie., 1873), 10, 20.
8. As quoted in Albert E. Stone's *The Innocent Eye: Childhood in Mark Twain's Imagination,* 210.
9. Ibid.

final authority rests, he leaves us with Alden/Twain and his "own word alone."

A fictive translator interpreting an imaginary narrator along a fancifully curbed road seems to mock the scholarly pretensions of the list of authorities following the title page. However, Twain did rely upon these authorities for the "truthfulness" of his own narrative, and to subvert that truth entirely would mean he would undermine the credibility of his own word. It is much more likely he was mocking traditional modes of making authoritative claims in general and any pretensions they may make to having the final word on any facts. Allowing anyone to claim finality would bring truth's verifying process to a halt. The truth that matters, truth in the making, would cease. In effect, Twain's opening strategy redistributes authority itself; the front matter becomes a paradoxical truth-making event that encourages readerly participation. His ludic handling of historical claims enhances our awareness of our own part in the negotiation of those claims; at the same time, it trains us to think independently and to determine true ideas apart from textual constraints.

This parodic undermining of textual authority finds its place in what Richard Rorty defines as an ironical attempt to unmask confidence in "final vocabularies" within truth's verification process. I would not completely situate Twain within Rorty's definition of an "ironist," one who is "never quite able to take" himself or his language seriously because of an awareness of the "contingency and fragility" of both. However, Twain's portrait of Joan does partake in that act of "redescription" Rorty defines as the ironist's attempt to free us from "incarnated vocabularies," the words through and in which our very identity hardens.[10] Although Twain argued for the contingency of language and truth in *Joan of Arc,* he would never limit the imagination or its part in realizing one's freedom to the confines of language. Twain's description of Joan's religious experiences, in fact, suggests the possibility of an understanding beyond the margins of verbal awareness.

Within the confines of language, of course, ironists can only offer more words as they play one authoritative vocabulary against another; nonetheless, by comparing and contrasting the descriptions and redescriptions of authorized final claims, they open the necessary

10. Richard Rorty, *Contingency, Irony, and Solidarity,* 74.

dialectical space for verifying the truest of experiences. Therefore, Twain's fancy work in the opening pages works not only to set the stage for a textual presentation of his idea of truth as process but it also clears the decks for a newly imagined discourse that reflects this validating process and hence empowers and authenticates the moment.

As he claims a right to imaginative reconstruction, Twain also follows a literary tradition. Poe claimed the same freedom in the prefatory pages of *The Narrative of Arthur Gordon Pym* where Pym, knowing the extravagances of his own "imaginative faculties," allows Poe to present his recollections of the "facts . . . under the garb of fiction." Pym, like Twain, leaves it up to the readers to sift for the bare facts through the "pretended fiction." The authorial "ruse" failed, however; as Pym explains, Poe's readers were determined to read his fiction as fact. Seeing no need to continue on with their ingenious plan, both he and Poe decided to coauthor the writing of his narrative. He trusts that his readers will perceive the difference between Poe's fictional and his own factual account of the truth. Similarly, Hawthorne prefaces *The Blithedale Romance* by explaining that the facts are "altogether incidental" in terms of the "improved effects" produced by the romance. Melville, too, questions the validity of "received" experience in a similar fashion as he introduces *Moby-Dick*. Before quoting several pages of testimony to the character and true history of the "leviathan," he warns that they represent "higgledy-piggledy" scholarship at best, and "however authentic" it is, it must not be taken for "veritable gospel cetology."[11] Such opening moves promise the truth while mocking all authoritative claims to it. Twain's front matter achieves a similar effect as it calls upon the reader to construct a usable truth, though Twain never quite dismisses fact's claim upon his own fancy work.

In his 1904 article on "Saint Joan of Arc," Twain asserts that Shakespeare's ignorance of the facts was responsible for his negative portrait of Joan in *Henry VI, Part I* (1592). Shakespeare's description of Joan as the "Foul fiend of France, and hag of all despite," as a tawdry peasant lost within the arms of "lustful paramours," reflects the hostile literary and historical treatment of Joan that began with

11. Edgar Allan Poe, *The Narrative of Arthur Gordon Pym*, 44, Nathaniel Hawthorne, *The Blithedale Romance*, 1–2, and Herman Melville, *Moby-Dick*, 2.

the English-aligned Burgundians, who depicted Joan as a "very cruel woman," in league with the devil and a "murderer of Christian people."[12] In his *Chronicles of England,* William Caxton continued to build upon this image of cruelty, describing Joan as little more than a criminal and adding his own particularly defamatory suggestion: "And then she said that she was with child, but in conclusion, it was found that she was not with child, and then she was burnt in Rouen." Caxton's odd inclusion of this unfounded assertion worked to undermine Joan's honesty and, at the same time, opened the way for later attacks upon her famed virginity. This speculation, however hastily retracted, became fact for many; in his *Chronicles* in 1587, Holinshed presented Joan as a young strapping wench, whose "devilish practices" and impurity stained her own "dignity" along with that of France.[13]

For Twain, the most reliable record of Joan was the French tradition that extended back along the path leading to the early chronicles. The chronicles began as journal or diary notes by those who were personally involved with Joan during her battles but were supplemented by other accounts before being published as distinct narratives. The *Journal of the Siege of Orleans,* for example, was not completed until 1467, though most of its details were written in 1428 while Joan was still commanding her army. It was not published until 1896. Twain would have had access to passages from the chronicles through Quicherat, though only in their modern French translation. Written by those who were either directly connected with Joan or had access to firsthand accounts of her military ventures, these accounts document a brave and patriotic Joan, that heroic and virtuous image reaffirmed in the official records of Joan's rehabilitation.[14]

12. Frances Gies, *Joan of Arc: The Legend and the Reality,* 240–42. While Gies's book builds its own portrait of Joan through a synthesis of known fact and written accounts, I am particularly indebted to her chapter titled "Five and a Half Centuries of Joan of Arc" for my own overview of the history of Joan's reception and representation.
13. Ibid., 44–45. Joan's image was divided along political lines from the beginning. During Joan's rehabilitation process, Joan's confessor recalled how Joan would herself cry over the epithet the English had chosen for her: the "Armagnac's whore." See Jewkes, *Joan of Arc,* 67.
14. My information on the chronicles is taken from Ingvald Raknem's *Joan of Arc in History, Legend and Literature,* 4. Raknem provides a useful list of hundreds of works pertaining to Joan of Arc, starting from Christine de Pisan's unti-

This portrait was kept alive through the centuries primarily by the very Church that burned her and yet also authenticated the records documenting her purity. In Joan's own century, Pope Pius II (1458–1464), in his notes on the history of the fifteenth century, declared that "no breath of scandal was ever heard" concerning Joan of Arc, and that in commanding an army of men she "kept her purity unstained" in their company (Gies, 247). Pius II, however, started his own rumor by suggesting that Joan's miracles may have been staged by French leadership to inspire the French people, whose patriotism had been faltering.[15] Although Joan's image suffered from eighteenth-century skeptical pens, French Revolutionary writers, who were less interested in her purity than in her strength and courage, troped her into the voice of the radical patriot and, for many, France itself. As she dramatically broke through her oppressive layers of chains in the conclusion of Friedrich Schiller's *Die Jungfrau von Orleans,* first performed in 1801, Joan arrived in the nineteenth century as the "lion-hearted maid" and the incarnation of freedom itself.

This is the image upon which Twain chose to build. Schiller's play was a favorite of Twain and his family and even as late as 1906 he quoted it in a telling autobiographical entry. Despairing of those surrounding Joan, Twain records Schiller's line, "Against the stupid even the gods strive in vain."[16] Given his research and extensive reading, Twain may very well have believed himself to be struggling against a history of stupidity. As he explained in an essay originally written as an introduction to an English translation of the official documents surrounding the trial and rehabilitation process of Joan of Arc, for him, Joan of Arc was a "miracle-working new breath of Liberty" blown upon an oppressed people. This is the "vision" he wished to deliver artistically, in order to "win us" over to "the light of that lustrous intellect and the fires of that unquenchable spirit" Twain knew as Joan of Arc.[17]

---

tled lyrics in praise of Joan (1429–1430) and extending to the plays of George Bernard Shaw and Bertolt Brecht.

15. Gies, *Joan of Arc: The Legend and the Reality,* 247.

16. See Gribben, *Mark Twain's Library,* 606.

17. Mark Twain, "Saint Joan of Arc," 158–59. As Paine explains in the *Biography,* however, Twain, who rarely accepted criticism gracefully, withdrew his introductory essay after the editor, whom he saw as summarily a "long-eared animal" and "literary kangaroo," an "illiterate hostler with his head full of axle-grease," attempted to alter his ideas (1091).

Yet Twain does not try to sell a pig in a poke. His juggling of fact and fiction in the front matter demands a participatory and hence critical role for the reader, whose own process of sifting truth and fact mirrors the truth-as-process that Twain then embodies in his plot. Juxtaposing the "vocabularies of alternative figures," to recall Rorty's description of an ironist, Twain leads us into "alternative redescriptions" of historical fact, images of reality upon which we may choose "to re-create ourselves, in whole or in part."[18] Twain's ironical treatment of the finality of authority therefore also includes self-parody as it perforce reflects back upon himself as well as his fictive translator.

Although his front matter deflates all traditional (rhetorical) pretensions to authority, implicitly even his own, Twain nevertheless attempts to deliver a persuasively commanding portrait. Richard Poirier says that such a text "shapes itself around its own dissolvents"; he also describes the workings of a "literature of self-parody" that mocks all attempts to authorize "*articulated* forms of life or reality or history" as conclusively true.[19] However, the recognition of truth's corruptibility through "human contrivance," or human articulation, does not relieve literature from its duty to contrive articulately. Poirier defines such work as literature's only "responsibility," a work that allows the writer the freedom of loosely attending to what he calls the "alternative inventions" of "history, life, reality, or politics" as long as the writing itself is "compelled and compelling about its own inventions."[20] Twain was certainly driven by the energy of his own creation. Like another compulsively inventive mind—William James's—Twain accepted the provisional fictionality of truth, as his prefatory pages attest, without "backing out and crying 'no play'" (*Pragmatism*, 132).

Both Twain and James in this sense prefigure what Poirier points to as a typically modern parody of received and accepted truths and meaning by writers "burdened with the wastes of time" and "cultural shards and rubbish." However, in their continued attempt to shape a reality upon such shards, they define themselves as less allied with their traditional counterparts than attached to a shared pragmatistic

---

18. Rorty, *Contingency, Irony, and Solidarity*, 80.
19. Richard Poirier, *The Performing Self: Compositions and Decompositions in the Languages of Contemporary Life*, 27–28.
20. Ibid., 31.

vision.[21] That is to say, Twain and James belonged to the nineteenth century and, under the influence of a lingering Emersonian transcendentalism, still believed in the transformative power of thought and language. To be sure, they realized the fictionality of the truths in which humans find their existence, as Twain to some degree reveals in his dismantling of narrative authority. At the same time, though, they were far from considering their efforts to create realities as futile. This, too, is moral idealism, and it functions in tandem with the recognition of truth's contingency; it enabled Twain, in particular, to work through the depiction of vicissitudes of thought and language in his novel, reflecting the life of ideas in his *Joan of Arc* as true in a newer and fresher sense.

The kinds of experience that function as truth within Twain's portrait of Joan, finding their markers in such traditional terms as virtue, courage, and patriotism, verify and promote the most existentially central avenues of freedom and liberty. These are vital paths to a set of actions that not only provided Twain with images through and by which to authenticate Joan's thought, but also through which he could continue developing his psychology of the divided self. Such a psychology both allows for and denies that independence of mind that Twain wished to celebrate through his portrait of Joan. Such a paradoxical understanding of the self points to the contradictory nature of Twain's metaphysics and his ongoing ambivalence concerning the self's essential condition, whether it be free or determined. In particular, the question of the will's freedom and its function within thought and action would always be one that would philosophically divide Twain's own sensibilities; the division seems especially poignant in his attempts to promote independent thought. Although both he and James worked to provoke others into thinking for themselves, Twain was never as certain as James appeared to be about the human capacity to think and act freely. Even in the case of James, it often appears that his need to defend the will's freedom, a need that finds a central place of expression within all his major works, reveals a recurring doubt about its actual existential possibility.

It is clear that Twain and James were not alone in their uncertainties, either before or after the century's turn. However, in their con-

21. Ibid., 33.

tinuing efforts to authenticate an autonomous self, one essential to that Jamesian pragmatism that finds its locus of power within individual thought, both men sought to deploy the creative force they felt inherent within that ideal, even when moving against an apparently overwhelming tendency toward determinism. This conflict between the claims of freedom and those of determinism had surfaced earlier in *Huckleberry Finn* dividing Twain's realistic treatment of life along the Mississippi from his inward turn into his hero's consciousness. Huck's inner journey had not only provided Twain with a means for exploring the workings of consciousness, but also allowed him to describe an alternative world structured around the possibility of ideal action, action that implicitly pointed to a higher order of reality and to the spiritually renewing effect to be had through its experience. Twain's attempt to imagine such a world against the demands of the more modern mode of realism practiced by many of his contemporaries, moreover, partially accounts for the contradictory impulses that continue to find their expression in *Joan of Arc*.

Jackson Lears, in his study of American culture between 1880 and 1920, locates such imaginative efforts within an "antimodernist" protest against the spiritual vacuity of an ever-encroaching modern culture. Situating this protest primarily among middle- and upper-class reformers and intellectuals, Lears provides a complex analysis of a particular American response to a cultural "drift toward weightlessness," an increasing tendency to cast overboard the ballast of significant moral and spiritual beliefs. Lears's useful approach to American antimodernism prevents us from narrowly defining its causes or expression, but he indeed suggests that a "religious disquiet lay at the root of all the profounder varieties of antimodernism," reflecting a "vein of deep religious longing, an unfulfilled yearning to restore infinite meaning to an increasingly finite world."[22] Just as pertinent to my argument is that Lears centers much of this antimodernist reaction on the "free will–determinism debate." Lears points out that for some, such as Henry Adams, only faith could resolve the debate. James had argued for such a faith in "The Will to Believe," but his belief went beyond recognizing the "hopelessness" of the "human condition" to positing the shape of "infinite meaning" within the purview of belief.

22. T. J. Jackson Lears, *No Place of Grace: Antimodernism and the Transformation of American Culture, 1880–1920*, 45.

Lears, however, questions the possible motive behind such faith and points to the possible link between corporate aims and the "rhetoric of liberation." He also reads *Joan of Arc* suspiciously, and considers Twain's Joan to be primarily an "emblem of nationalism sanctified by religiosity."[23] However, I am not so sure as Lears that Twain sacrificed Joan's private self and her inward turnings to a demanding public display of national pride. Rather, the writing of *Joan of Arc* allowed Twain to further consider and confess his faith in the hypothetical case for independent thought and action he had offered through the character of Huckleberry Finn.

Both Twain and James, then, found their own place in this anti-modernist discontent, and, as Lears himself argues, their beliefs and religious yearnings found fulfillment through a psychology that included a metaphysics of freedom. James explained as much in his *Psychology;* he chose the "alternative of freedom," an alternative so compelling that for him the freedom of the will was to become his "settled creed" (2:573). Although Twain would never declare freedom as a fixed reality and never remove his deterministic doubts from the dialectical play of his texts, his major works nonetheless speak for his own choice of freedom as the core condition of human thought and action. Freedom in this sense would be a self-determining process that not only shaped the fate of human progress in the world but actually created the world through which we progress.

Twain's development of this spiritual or religious psychology, however, could never wholly discount the autonomous claims of a "finite world," even when positing infinitely creative powers within the range of human consciousness. Although his opening strategy frees his subject from strict historical terms, his text proper continues to work within those terms through the recollections of his narrator. Through his use of the Sieur Louis de Conte, Twain continues to verify the truth of his idea of freedom-as-process even against his own deterministic forebodings. His complex use of de Conte as an essentially unreliable narrator, at the same time, allows him to speak both for and against his own doubts and beliefs.

De Conte can be "both blunt and gentle, pious and anticlerical, cynical and awestruck," exhibiting those "twin tendencies toward sentimentality and realism" that Albert Stone claims characterizes "vir-

23. Ibid., 54, 152.

tually all of Twain's fiction."[24] As Stone points out, this double perspective worked well for Twain in his earlier apprenticeship works
such as *Roughing It* and "Old Times on the Mississippi"; as an old
man recalling his adventures with Joan, de Conte can speak as both
a naive youth, full of hope and faith, and as a weathered cynic,
embittered by experience. However, Stone is wrong when he says
that "the page speaks for his creator" or, in other words, that he is
"Twain's alter ego."[25] To align Twain's view wholly with de Conte's
perspective would be to miss the point of Twain's prefatory strategy,
and of his dismantling of any one authoritative point of view.

On the other hand, entirely discounting de Conte's authority, as
Christina Zwarg does in her deconstructive, feminist reading of *Joan
of Arc,* severs an important tie to the experience Twain wishes to verify. Zwarg does present an interesting argument defending Twain's
Joan of Arc against its harsh reception among modern critics. Zwarg
maintains that Twain's novel continues to be read as a failure because
critics have failed to recognize "feminist concerns" in "American
thought" in general. Zwarg contends that the authoritative terms of a
primarily masculine critical perspective have caused Joan of Arc to be
written "out of history," and critics who deny this are reenacting the
"patriarchal" inscribing of Joan's life that Twain attempts to dismiss.
Twain shows himself as a proto-feminist with this novel, but his "critique of phallocentrism," as Zwarg calls it, does not thoroughly dismantle de Conte's authority, discounting entirely the "work of historian, poet, and storyteller alike" through him.[26] Twain was a pragmatist in the Jamesian mold, and his deconstructive inclinations were
more than balanced by his constructive ones, his choices to build
upon history in order to reconfigure and revitalize its core truths.

Twain, in other words, arguably continued his fancy work on both
sides of the historical road, employing images of both medieval and
modern mentalities in his revisionist project. De Conte may be both

24. Albert E. Stone, *The Innocent Eye: Childhood in Mark Twain's
Imagination,* 213.

25. Stone, 211–13.

26. Christina Zwarg, "Woman as Force in Twain's Joan of Arc: The
Unwordable Fascination," 57, 60. The debate over Joan's image continues as,
curiously enough, Stone equates Twain with his narrator because he claims to
"teach" the important facts of history, while Zwarg points to this pedagogical
intent as the object of Twain's derision.

an object of Twain's parodic aim and a reliable link to the facts, a means through which Twain continued his prefatory strategy of pluralizing the truth as he juggles the facts between de Conte's fifteenth-century report and his own nineteenth-century perception of them. However, instead of completely denying the validity of de Conte's recollections, this juggling loosens only our sense of narrative control, and so continues to validate the experience of freedom within and outside of particular experiential horizons and governing expectations. This juggling through differing perspectives or expectations emerges with particular force within the descriptions of Joan's religious experiences and, in fact, begins with some of Twain's most fanciful work: his use and abuse of Domremy's magical tree.

The Fairy Tree and Angelic Calls

Testimony at Joan's trial attests to an old beech tree that stood at the edge of town and was believed to have been the haunt of magical fairies in earlier pagan times. Still believing the tree to possess mystical powers, the Church had appropriated the tree for its own use in Joan's day, sanctioning the Christian celebrations and festivals held beneath its branches. Like most people in her village, Joan had participated in these festivities. Little more is known about Domremy's fairy tree and it appears in the trial records only as background information on Joan's childhood. Little notice, in fact, is given to it by any of the narratives working from those records—until Twain's.

Twain would have found testimony about this magical tree in Quicherat's translation of the trial records, where Joan's godmother explains that "fees [fairies], or "ladies that cast spells," frequented the area around the tree.[27] Twain, however, was not willing to allow the Church to absorb the lore of the fairy tree, along with the supernatural powers associated with it, into its own. Rather, he set the Church in conflict with the power of the tree, and thus against Joan, who plays within its shadow.

He begins early in *Joan of Arc* setting forth this contrast between her vision and that of the institutional Church by attaching a legend of his own fabrication to the fairy tree, describing the "mystic privi-

27. Gies, *Joan of Arc: The Legend and the Reality,* 21–22.

lege" granted to those who frequented it (1:26). Those who believed in the tree's powers, he suggests, were allowed to see it one last time before their death, if all were well with their souls, and if they did see the tree, it was a divine sign that assured their own redemption. The tree would appear to the believers "as through a rift in a cloud that curtains heaven," an opening through which, according to de Conte, "the soft picture of the Fairy Tree, clothed in a dream of golden light" with the "bloomy mead sloping away to the river" appears as a "vision" promising paradise to the "sinless dying forlorn" (1:27).

Twain's elaboration of the inherited folklore here allows him the opportunity of separating his own use of the motif from that of his narrator. De Conte uses the experience primarily to claim his own sanctity, for he has "seen the vision" and awaits his heavenly reward. Twain similarly blesses Joan with this "special grace"; he depicts her standing "forlorn" in a dungeon cell in the last days of her life, "a poor friendless thing," though having seen the vision assured heaven (2:297). His perspective is singled out as particularly medieval, at least as Twain depicts it, for de Conte can only locate the tree's importance within a specific Christian cosmology of the cross, one paralleling the actual appropriation of the tree's supposed mystic powers by the Church in Domremy. His vision of the tree thus finds its end and beginning in the sacrifice and redemption of a Christian god. Twain's authorial uses of the tree's "apparition" suggest another source and literary use, for the dream imagery that accompanies de Conte's descriptions also points to Twain's ongoing interest in psychic phenomena in general and in the nature and function of dreams in particular.

The "apparition" of the tree comes in a "dream of golden light," to return to de Conte's description, or as a "soft picture" while one is apparently entranced. The dream imagery is further enhanced by the phrase "bloomy mead." Its associated meanings suggest the feeling of bodily release effected by drinking alcohol or perhaps the haze following such imbibing, while in a more poetic sense, the phrase evokes the lyric world of meadows full of blossoms, which is still suggestive of the vividness of color experienced in dreams. As Joan drinks in her own vision, imprisoned in the dungeon's darkness, we find her "lost in dreams and thinkings" (2:297). Twain could not invest in that childlike faith in Christian mythology shared by the

"Children of the Tree," a faith de Conte claims for both himself and Joan, but Twain could invest modestly in the comfort and strength that they apparently found in their beliefs. His own late-nineteenth-century mind would need to posit most of his faith in the self's ability to envision and enact its own divine potential, its own liberating dream. Twain's version of the apparition of the fairy tree, as deployed in his text, argues for that envisioning power, for a human capacity for a mystical or religious experience in self-generating authenticity. He would continue to link Joan's documented visions and voices to the interior life of dream as psychic phenomena.

The trial records richly document Joan's urgent and steady claim to divinely inspired experiences, and the Church's relentless probing into the question of their legitimacy. Her inquisitors were especially concerned about her "Voices." Joan had repeatedly explained that the voices came when she was just thirteen, the first one being that of St. Michael, the archangel, who had appeared with a host of angels and the intense "spiritual light" that would most always accompany her visitations. "I saw them with my bodily eyes as well as I see you," she told the court, which was proof enough for Joan that the commands they delivered were as God's own and that was all the authority she needed for her actions.[28] But it was also all the Church needed to condemn Joan, for she was challenging its own authority and claiming a share of its power.

Twain made a great deal of literary hay with this confrontation. His Chaucerian description of Bishop Cauchon, for example, might stand for Twain's dominant line on the Church itself: "obese" and "puffing and wheezing," de Conte describes him, "his great belly distending and receding with each breath" and "his three chins" rolling beneath his "knobby and knotty face" with its "purple and splotchy complexion, and his repulsive cauliflower nose, and his cold and malignant eyes" (2:141). As mentioned before, however, Twain could not fully credit Joan's personal faith in the origin of her visions. In the margins of one of his examined sources, he had noted the inanity of its writer who could still "in the 19th century" believe in the reality of angels. For his part, as he explains in defining his own deistic creed, Twain could believe in God but not in a God that spoke to anyone or "ever

28. Jewkes, *Joan of Arc: Fact, Legend, and Literature,* 12–13.

sent a message to man by anybody."[29] His narrator could, however, and indeed de Conte claims to have been present during Joan's visitations and to have personally witnessed the miraculous apparitions so essential to her mission.

Coming upon Joan while she sat beneath the "haunted beech tree," de Conte sets the mood for her mystic experience:

> The day was overcast, and all that grassy space wherein the Tree stood lay in a soft rich shadow. Joan sat on a natural seat formed by gnarled great roots of the Tree. Her hands lay loosely, one reposing in the other, in her lap. Her head was bent a little toward the ground, and her air was that of one who is lost in thought, steeped in dreams, and not conscious of herself or of the world. (1:86)

We cannot be sure whether she was praying, reflecting, meditating, or dreaming, or just lost in intense introspection, though de Conte assures us he himself witnessed the events that follow. He saw a "white shadow come gliding along the grass toward the Tree," a "robed form—with wings" and "whiteness of lightnings," whose "brilliancy was so blinding," as de Conte recalls, "that it pained my eyes and brought water into them" (1:86–87). Slowly this transfigurative shade of white light envelops Joan herself:

> The shadow approached Joan slowly, the extremity of it reached her, flowed over her, clothed her in its awful splendor. In that immortal light her face, only humanly beautiful before, became divine; flooded with that transforming glory her mean peasant habit was become like to the raiment of the sun-clothed children of God as we see them thronging the terraces of the Throne in our dreams and imaginings. (1:87)

Once again, de Conte reveals the limits of his own imagination. It is not that the figure he draws lacks imagination: his description of

---

29. The source is Monseigneur Ricard's *Jeanne d'Arc la Vénérable,* 23, Mark Twain Papers. Twain's deistic beliefs are set forth in what Paul Baender has entitled "Three Statements of the Eighties" in *What Is Man? and Other Philosophical Writings,* 57–59. Twain often accepted the views of his Catholic sources, however, as his comments within their works attest.

Joan's glorified countenance rivals that of the visionary St. John in expressive power. Instead, it is his use of readily available biblical images to interpret this shadowy illumination that clearly reveals the limiting lens through which he reads Joan's actions.

Twain's use of a double simile in the mouth of his narrator, on the other hand, allows him to balance the presentation between what it may be "like" and "how" it might be read, leaving us to believe or not believe in divine intervention, or rather in "dreams and imaginings," or some combination thereof. Without becoming overinsistent, Twain uses a similar image in *No. 44, The Mysterious Stranger,* portraying No. 44 in "unearthly splendor" and "supernal beauty," within the rays of a "flooding light" and "clothed" in "immortal fire, and flashing like the sun."[30] His use of such vivid imagery in both *No. 44* and *Joan of Arc* reveals, among other things, a belief in the existence of a superior, if not divine, "dream self." More to the point, Twain's inclusion of the vision of the tree and de Conte's eyewitness report affirm the human capacity for religious experiences, yet the nature of these experiences remains open for discussion. This is another way of saying that Twain accepted the truth of the experiences but not his narrator's reading of them. The truth for Twain, and a no less liberating or empowering one, is that by definition visions exist only in the processes of mind, and we need not look further for the reality of religious experiences or for any external verification of their worth.

In *The Varieties of Religious Experiences,* James provides another useful lens for reading Twain's decentering (though not annihilation) of textual authority. Although not published until 1902, the *Varieties* articulates speculations, made over many years, about psychic phenomena. Indeed James classifies religious experiences as examples of those extraordinary mentations both he and Twain would have known through their psychical research. However, he did not wish to deny religious experiences their spiritual or revelatory significance; instead, he sought to understand their significance and worth in terms of a "wider scope" of "human experience" (*Varieties,* 30). Regardless of their source, the experiences were real and, as such, were worth examining for their effects upon the collection of truths constitutive of reality.

30. Mark Twain, *No. 44, The Mysterious Stranger,* 390.

Joan of Arc was a prime candidate for such investigations. And here we might recall Lears and his study of antimodernism. As Lears points out, in protesting a "desanctified, weightless universe," antimodernists often turned toward "medieval mentalities" for a "range of imagination and emotional life" they believed was missing in modern society, a move he sees "at bottom" as a compelling "religious impulse" or "longing to locate some larger purpose in a baffling universe."[31] I would add that in their turning inward, both James and Twain were driven by a desire to locate the springs of creativity as much as by their need to identify with a larger power. Although Twain may have attempted to extend the reach of his imagination through his portrait of Joan, he turned to her at the same time for further investigations and attempts to deny or verify paranormal activity and individual claims to exceptional mental states.

The records document not only Joan's voices and visions but also those psychical abilities central to the research of the S.P.R. and its members: mental telepathy, precognition, and clairvoyance. Three "peculiarities," as Quicherat had described them before the advent of a theory or vocabulary that might explain them psychologically, are on record in support of such psychic power: her ability to read the king's mind upon initially meeting him, her prophecy of her own injury at the battle of Orleans, and her knowledge and discovery of the sword she would carry into battle, a sword believed to have been Charlemagne's and found buried behind an altar in Fierbois. Whether we can scientifically account for these powers or not, as Quicherat concludes, they "must be admitted" as factual, and the voices and visions that enabled them as well, for no normal explanation can be given since "they seem to pass beyond the circle of human power."[32] Twain follows the documents in admitting all of these psychical "peculiarities" into his own narrative as well as adding another of his own, Joan's tendency to lapse unknowingly into trances.

This addition, and the veiling of Joan's visionary experience in dream imagery, links Twain's writing to his interest in the continuing investigations of the S.P.R. in general; in particular, it demonstrates the links to James's theory in *Varieties* of an "extra-marginal" field of con-

---

31. Lears, *No Place of Grace,* 181, 163, 181.
32. As quoted in appendix D to Andrew Lang's biography of Joan of Arc: *The Maid of France: Being the History of the Life and Death of Jeanne d'Arc,* 329–30.

sciousness (215). In admitting that there are transformative "forces seemingly outside of the conscious individual," James stressed that his psychology "diverges from Christian theology" only in the latter's insistence upon the "direct supernatural operations of the Deity" (196). Preferring to locate these forces within the individual mind, James theorized about an indeterminate margin of consciousness, one in which our entire "set of memories, thoughts, and feelings" continuously "floats beyond" our "primary consciousness," though "ready at touch to come in" (215). In varying combinations, the possibility of incursions of "residual powers, impulses, and knowledges" from this wider realm of being, or the "subliminal self," as James would come to use the term, points to unlimited creative sources within each individual.

Speculating along the same lines in his own articles on "mental telegraphy," Twain reported on both his own rare powers of mind along with the unusual abilities of others. The psychic phenomenon that would claim most of his attention, however, was the dream experience. However, Twain was not as certain as James that the subliminal self was a part of one's larger expanse of consciousness; in fact, he was developing his own theory of separate selves, entities encountered within our dreams or "trances" that in themselves were like waking dreams. In either phenomenon, the "dream self," as Twain understood it, emerges within as an independent agent with the "ordinary powers" of body and mind "enlarged in all particulars a little, and in some particulars prodigiously."[33] In "My Platonic Sweetheart" (1898), written a few years after the publication of *Joan of Arc* and during his early drafting of the *Mysterious Stranger Manuscripts,* Twain claimed even more for this "dream self." In this short essay the dream self is the "artist within us who constructs our dreams," who is "many hundreds of times the superior of the poor thing in us who architects our waking thoughts."[34] Twain's dream artist thus approaches more traditional senses of divinity itself, as he would affirm in his most ambitious portrayal of the dream self in *No. 44, The Mysterious Stranger.*

However, in his symbolic use of the vision of Domremy's fairy tree and in Joan's voices and visions that follow, his fusing of nar-

33. Twain, *Notebook,* 350.
34. Holograph Manuscript, Mark Twain Papers, Berkeley, pp. 15–16.

ratorial perspective within the suggestiveness of dream imagery reveals that Twain was not yet ready to posit a superior mind operating wholly and solely within the mechanisms of a dream self. Twain's presentation of Joan's visionary experiences, that is, refuses to deny completely the possible truth of his narrator's perspective. James explained that accepting an idea of a "subliminal self" does not necessarily mean rejecting the notion of divine intervention; in the same vein, Twain's narrative juggles between fact and fiction and allows for either a theological or psychological interpretation. "Just as our primary wide-awake consciousness throws open our senses to the touch of things material, so it is logically conceivable that if there be higher spiritual agencies that can directly touch us," as James suggests, "the psychological condition of their doing so might be our possession of a subconscious region" that keeps "ajar" the "door" to the "dreamy Subliminal" (223). By hanging the "door" between himself and his narrator, Twain allows the hinges to swing both ways. As a contemporary witness, de Conte opens the door into a particular medieval view; in presenting his distant testimony, Twain swings the door wider for a greater access to a more modern truth within the reality of religious experience.

The situation for Twain, as for James, is that the self is potentially free and is capable of a range of thought and action apparently outside normal limitations. Joan of Arc was living proof of this potential freedom, one leading to the "untried capacities" within each individual, according to Twain, of a freedom little used by the majority of the human race.[35] Joan's voices and visions were on record as historical fact, but freedom itself, like any word, remains dead apart from its life as continued engagement and self-verification in human affairs.

Liberating Voices

Returning to James's theory of truth's verifying process, we can now see how Twain's narrative, like his prefatory pages, partakes in and also reflects the process itself. His juggling of narrative perspective, in particular, provides a literary image of evolving relations between truth and fact mediated by the mind. James explains that the function

35. Twain, "Saint Joan of Arc," 155.

of this node of relationships relies as much upon one's search for and ultimate faith in the truth as upon one's knowledge of the facts:

> So the whole coil and ball of truth, as it rolls up, is the product of a double influence. Truths emerge from facts; but they dip forward into facts again and add to them; which facts again create or reveal new truth (the word is indifferent) and so on indefinitely. The "facts" themselves are meanwhile not *true*. They simply *are*. Truth is the function of the beliefs that start and terminate among them. (*Pragmatism*, 101)

Our participation in crafting reality through "successive pushes" of ideas or beliefs upon the body of facts is, as James draws the analogy, similar to a "snowball's growth." To use another Jamesian figure, "beliefs at any time are so much experience *funded*"; as such, they "become matter, therefore, for the next day's funding operations" (*Pragmatism*, 101). Therefore, as we fund an experience, truth, or reality, grows out from our ideas about it or, to be more precise, truths are inextricably bound up with our use of the facts and the beliefs we forge between and among them.

This idea of funding beliefs can be clarified as we consider Joan's capacity for the kind of heroic action that complements her religious experiences and so embodies her freedom in Twain's terms. We begin by giving further attention to James's market metaphor of funding. By troping the whole stream of historical experience into the image of an investment fund, one in which we profit both from previous deposits and future returns, James exemplifies the funding process itself as a proto-social psychology. Like Emerson's "market metaphors," which, as Richard Poirier points out, are "scarcely meant to suggest that we are merely pawns of overdetermined categories," James's metaphor loosens the "restrictive" bonds of the "language of finance and economy," returning the words themselves back into the flow of a wider human commerce. Ideas and beliefs by necessity are primarily funded through language, and "what James says of beliefs," as Poirier notes, "is even more the case with words, as they "are themselves parts of the sum total of the world's experience."[36] Insofar as language represents this experiential sum, then, its "funding oper-

---

36. Richard Poirier, *Poetry and Pragmatism*, 97, 137.

ations," to recast James's words, require a continual reworking of our vocabulary, which effectively shapes our future experience and our sense of the reality of that experience. To extend the point further, the reality of "being" itself is shaped more or less through the funding of language. Twain claims as much in his mocking of the words of inherited authority in his prefatory matter.

The idea that identity, like history, is to a large extent contingent upon language echoes an "age-old skepticism," as Poirier points out, one that continues to inform the postmodern moment. But where both Twain and James differ from many skeptical postmoderns is in their pragmatist "belief that language, and therefore thinking, can be changed by an individual's acts of imagination and by an individual's manipulation of words."[37] Returning words that have been preempted by special interests, in particular, back into the general discourse of words becomes James's small way of recuperating and rehabilitating the very terms upon which we continue to build the self. What becomes necessary, then, is not the acquisition of new words but a repossession of those already in stock, a redirecting of that vital energy languishing within deadening conceptions and, in effect, a reclamation of the self that stands ready for future funding.

This brings us back again to the problem of *freedom* and its meaning in *Joan of Arc;* both the word and Joan herself merge throughout the text, and to define one means, in large part, to know the other. Through a continued juggling of narrative control, as with Joan's visionary experiences, Twain allows the complementary play of words and images to have a revisioning effect. This process realigns the word *freedom* within both Joan's spiritual experience and her heroic, political, and military action.

Beginning in the first chapter, de Conte narrowly defines Joan and the freedom she embodies within the French Armagnac cause. Like himself, de Conte explains that Joan and "every human creature in the village" of Domremy was "an Armagnac—a patriot," faithful to King and Church and sworn enemies of the English and their French sympathizers, the Burgundians (1:22). For the Armagnacs, liberty and patriotism were synonymous; de Conte insists that Joan was "*the* Patriot" among patriots (1:53). She was the embodiment of freedom, moreover, and for de Conte this meant France incarnate,

37. Ibid., 135.

an image worthy of not only reverence but also worship. After attempting to construct this image throughout his recollections, de Conte concludes his narrative with the more brutal image of Joan wielding the "sword that severed her country's bonds" rather than the mind that might lead others to an independent selfhood. This is the image, and "no other," that de Conte insists ought to represent Joan for all time (2:318).

Such an idea is plausible enough for de Conte, who, like Joan, fought to liberate his country as an Armagnac and who, in writing after Joan's martyrdom, might be expected to lash out at those who had opposed their cause. However, de Conte's words in the novel are not left to stand as the final authority; just as Twain had earlier destabilized authorial truth-claims, so at the end he deflates his narrator's attempts to confine Joan to an Armagnac nationalistic vocabulary.

Ironically, de Conte's own patriotic fervor blinds him to the full meaning of Joan's visions and the experience of freedom she embodies. Letting his emotions get the best of him, de Conte undermines his own attempts to correlate freedom and patriotism as he leads us through one of Joan's particularly devastating attacks:

> Joan of Arc raised her sword in the air. At the signal the silence was torn to rags; cannon after cannon vomited flames and smoke . . . and a startled girl dropped her water pot and clasped her hands together, [as] a stone cannonball crashed through her fair body [as] the great artillery duel went on, each side hammering away with all its might; and it was splendid for smoke and noise, and most exalting to one's spirits. (1:341)

"Great," "splendid," and "exalting" are adjectives that link de Conte more to Twain's conquering Yankee Hank Morgan, whose own adrenaline would rise with a vast display of force, than to Joan of Arc. However, just as he satirically both reflects and undermines the Yankee's heroic fervor at the end of *A Connecticut Yankee*, Twain mocks de Conte's own patriotic fever and irrational nationalism.

We watch de Conte undermine the patriotism he would have us believe to be Joan's own as he moves beyond his already questionable martial exuberance to a pathological barbarism of sorts. "Soldiering makes few saints," he tells us, after he and his cohort find pleasure in the misery of the prisoners they have taken (2:48). As he eggs the same prisoners on into fighting among themselves, de

Conte's passions are aroused by the "death shrieks" and the spurting of "brilliant artery blood," after which he concludes that the whole affair provided "one of the pleasantest incidents of my checkered military career" (2:48). Human suffering and insensitivity toward it appalled Twain, and we might read de Conte's gleeful comments, given the ironies in the narrative voice behind *Joan of Arc,* as both sincere and sardonic. Indeed, Twain's aged narrator has reason enough to deride his youthful and fanatical devotion to a cause that would ultimately lead his beloved Joan to a miserable end.

Joan, herself, according to documented testimony, regretted the pain and suffering issuing from her battles. As Jean d'Aulon testified during Joan's rehabilitation process, she would often weep and pray over the dead after a battle, both her own country's and the dead among the enemy.[38] Therefore, though de Conte presents a part of that spirit of liberty that Twain himself feels essential to any portrayal of Joan—she did resist the tyranny of her country's oppressors through armed force—at the same time he reveals in his narrator the moral bankruptcy of the tyranny of absolute ideals and unchanging truths.

Such patriotic ideals can become our "true lords," as James pointed out in *Varieties,* and take the place and fulfill the function of God and religion as "enlargers of our life" (251); however, like the "fruits of religion" and "all human products," as James continued to explain in his chapter "The Value of Saintliness," idealistic devotion is "liable to corruption by excess" (310). De Conte's glee upon the sight of his enemies' blood certainly constitutes an excessive patriotic spirit, one that corrupts his own attitudes and thus his capacity to recognize the liberating experience Joan authenticates. De Conte is hardly Twain's ideal personality; he does not embody but rather points to the ideal; his "devotional recollections," to recall James's words, are more likely to reveal the truth by distorting it.

Applying his psychology to saintly character, James detailed the dangers of pursuing ideality:

> Strong affections need a strong will; strong active powers need a strong intellect, strong intellect needs strong sympathies to keep life steady. If the balance exist, no one faculty can possibly

---

38. See Jewkes, *Joan of Arc: Fact, Legend, and Literature,* 62.

be too strong—we only get the stronger all-round character. . . .
Spiritual excitement takes pathological forms whenever other
interests are too few and the intellect too narrow. (310)

In Jamesian terms, de Conte's patriotic fervor undergirds his own
pathological behavior; it is characteristically ironic that Twain's village
scholar emerges with an intellect too narrow to comprehend the
essential meaning behind Joan's struggle for freedom.

For Twain, however, Joan's affections find a balance within the
operations of a "strong will" and "strong intellect." Within this balance, patriotic passion gains its meaning in a devotion to freedom as
an act of will, as a liberating phenomenon, rather than to a static idea
that defines the self within its own terms. All true beliefs, as Twain
wrote in a 1901 essay on patriotism, must be "reasoned out in a man's
own head and fire-assayed and tested and proved in his own conscience."[39] As with Huck Finn, Twain has Joan work through and
prove her own freedom in such a conscientious test. What he wants
to do is celebrate Joan's independence of mind by funding her capacity for independent thinking on the basis of human experience.

Joan's voices had come for four years before her decision to act
upon their urgings. At the age of thirteen, as she told her inquisitors
at her trial, the voices began to approach her with general instruc-
tions for the good of her own soul and with their first suggestions that
she would be the one to lead France to liberty. The voices continued,
urging her toward this end until she finally accepted her mission.
She is neither Paul, Francis, nor Theresa, as Lucien Fabre says in his
biography of Joan; her acceptance of the divine will came in stages
rather than in one radical submission to the piercing light of illumination. Her voices had to bargain their way into her mind. As Fabre
remarks, "it needed all the sweetness" and "diplomacy" of "two
saints" to "break her in by degrees to the idea" as France and heaven
waited for her to "make up her mind."[40] Whether heaven or Joan's
subliminal self was at work, compelling her through an impulsive
force, her actions also appear to have been derived from her own
conscious choice.

39. Mark Twain, "As Regards Patriotism," 45.
40. Lucien Fabre, *Joan of Arc,* 44.

Twain's definition of such a process of choice returns us to a passage from James's *Psychology* that had earler helped us gain a clearer understanding of Huck's decisive acts, where James described the "mental drama" as a "relation between the self" and its "states of mind" (2:564, 568). It is the possession of what James called the "effort-making capacity," a little-used capacity, he implied, and too often untried, to recall Twain's words. It is this capacity that leads to an intelligent, efficient, and orderly transition from thought to deed (1:126). As he discussed its central function within the movement of the will, James implied that effort lifts one above oneself. James said that effort moves us beyond those ideas and habits so ingrained as to constitute our realities; as we sacrifice these pleasurable ideas and soothing habits for "far-off considerations" or "unaccustomed reasons" through continued effort, we begin to invoke the potentially creative powers of the will (2:562–67). Our ideal motives or impulses, which, as James phrased it, arise like a "still small voice," will fade in impotence unless "artificially reinforced" through an increase in effort "to prevail" (2:549). The important point here is that James held the individual responsible for the forging of his or her reality, or, rather, he pointed to its necessary self-verification through the efforts of heroic minds. Further, he insisted that the locus of creation, potentially within the consciousness of each individual, turns with the will of the heroic mind out from its own deliberations.

Joan's voices came to her twice a week for four years and appeared to provoke her own reflective efforts while her will began its training. Even de Conte acknowledges Joan's thoughtful struggles, though his assurances that he alone could divine "her thinkings" set his authority up once again on dubious grounds (1:79). For a "whole year and a half" before her pivotal visitations, he explains, Joan "had been mainly grave: not melancholy, but given to thought, abstraction, dreams" (1:79). He assures us, as we might now expect, that her unusual self-absorption points to her patriotic devotion to France and the pain she suffered for its sake. De Conte's recounting of Joan's reaction to her voices suggests otherwise, however, as it reveals Joan struggling through the impositions of a heroic calling. Although he hears no angelic voices, he does hear Joan's pleas in response. "But I am so young," he recalls her saying, "so young to leave my mother and my home and go out into the strange world to undertake a thing so great!" Although Joan continues to throw her doubts about her mission into the open air—"How can I go to great wars, and lead armies?"—she finally yields to the commands she hears (1:88). In Jamesian terms, she consents to the reality of "far-off considerations" and thereby appropriates them. In doing so, she delivers herself over to the realization of a novel reality, or unaccustomed ideals, by means of her own efforts.

In his *Psychology,* James explained such an acceptance of a difficult action, even when it means facing death itself, as the result of sustained effort to keep the mind focused on the value of a given idea. The effort itself, as he pointed out in his chapter on the "Will," requires consent to the presence of an object in one's mind, until that object is "stably in possession of the field of one's thoughts," from which "it infallibly produces its own motor responses." The "attention must be kept strained on that one object," James continued, until at last it "fills" the mind, and this strain of attention is the fundamental act of the will. "Where the will is healthy," according to James, "the vision must be right . . . and the action must obey the vision's lead" (2:537). Joan's continual reflections, prayers, or introspective turnings, her clearing of initial obstructions, and her stilling of the dialectic within embody this Jamesian "healthy will." As we work within his terms, we find evidence to support a reading of her continuing efforts to maintain the presence of her voices as a gradual forging of her own inward freedom and authority. Such authority fuses her capacity for heroic action, or extraordinary effort, with her capacity for religious experience.

What makes James's description of this interior synthesis especially valuable here is Twain's own special interest in James's speculations. In his copy of the *Psychology,* Twain had been particularly drawn to the chapter "Habit" and its descriptive rationale for those "acquired aptitudes" that, according to James, "differ from instincts only in being prompted to action by the will" (1:117). This is an extremely important "only." Aside from asserting the very existence of the will as a separate faculty, James raised the will to a determining position apart from, though in tandem with, natural impulses. For James, the promptings of the will remain completely within one's own mental drama, and acquiring the ability to think for oneself is like reclaiming the truth within one's own being. The important point with which James concluded his chapter is that we can be taught to summon up this potential freedom by acquiring those habits essential to the functioning of a healthy will: the habits of "concentrated attention," of "energetic volition," and of "self-denial in unnecessary things" (1:127). Figuring his exemplary ideal of a balance of strong affections, intellect, and will in the ideal saintly personality, James offered these habits as a means toward effective use of these faculties for everyone.

Twain did something similar with his fictional account of the role habits play in significant action. Joan's continuing effort to fix her attention upon the calling of her voices, to work through and even question their divine authority, reveals her intellect at work as much as the pull of her affections. As Twain demonstrated repeatedly, even as his narrative leads Joan to the stake, her energetic use of will closely follows her efforts to concentrate upon her inner commands. De Conte notes the change in Joan's demeanor immediately following her pivotal submission to the archangel's command. "She moved and spoke with energy and decision," with "something wholly new and remarkable" about her person, proof for de Conte that God had invested her with his own "authority" (1:94–95). She carried herself without "ostentation or bravado," he later adds, and the "manifest sincerity and rocklike steadfastness of her convictions" surfaced in her very presence (1:113). Her physical endurance likewise reflected her powerful will, demonstrating to her page that "a great soul, with a great purpose," can indeed "make a weak body strong and keep it so" (1:208). Just as important for de Conte, the "valor-breeding inspiration of her name" alone could make other weak bodies strong, calling forth their own heroic capacities (1:256).

Heroic capacity, however, even as one continues his efforts to sacrifice the narrow interests of the self, can also lead to a pathological imbalance, to recall James's description, an imbalance exemplified in overweening affections, barren intellectual achievements, or the ruthless effects of a dominating will. These are not the experiences Twain, or James, wishes to fund. To remain engaged in authentic action means an ultimate disengagement of one's own self-gratifying desires and a denial of one's own demands, or commands, upon reality. Self-denial as a religious experience, moreover, requires a "surrender" of one's care for the self and a resigning of that care to "higher powers" (105–6). In spiritual terms, the will can only lead the self toward its expansive potential, the realization of this potential seemingly "left to other forces" that are evoked through the surrender of the will (194). However, in psychological terms, as James defined it in *Varieties,* the surrendering process can be seen as a cooperative effort of conscious and subliminal thought:

> A man's conscious wit and will, so far as they strain towards the ideal, are aiming at something only dimly and inaccurately imagined. Yet all the while the forces of mere organic ripening within him are going on towards their own prefigured result, and the conscious strainings are letting loose subconscious allies behind the scenes, which in their own way work towards rearrangement; and the rearrangement towards which all these deeper forces tend is pretty surely definite, and definitely different from what he consciously conceives and determines. It may consequently be actually interfered with (*jammed,* as it were, like the lost word when we seek too energetically to recall it), by his voluntary efforts slanting from the true direction. (194–95)

James's faith in the power of subliminal thought to carry us further than conscious deliberations points back to his theory of the "fringe," that whole of our "stream of thought" or entirety of experience that at any one time floats just beyond our current ideas. In partaking in this wider field of thought, a "penumbral" region of the mind providing seemingly infinite combinations of ideas, the subliminal self emerges, not surprisingly, as vastly superior to the self of the prosiac light of day.

Spiritual heroism, then, requires both a heroic effort of concentration, of directed and sustained thinking, and a willingness to submit one's stream of thought, one's known self, to the seemingly irrational compulsions of apparently superior forces. "To exercise the personal will" against such compelling forces, as James wrote later, in *Varieties,* "is still to live in the region where the imperfect self is the thing most emphasized"; when the "subconscious forces take the lead," as James explained, "it is more probably the better self *in posse* which directs the operation" (*Varieties,* 195). Thus an act of submission can be seen from this point of view as an act of liberation, a performance wholly within the mental drama and one enacting the mind's own freedom within its own play—though a degree of doubt, for the responsible mind, will also remain part of the calculus.

Joan's capacity for religious experience, as Twain suggests in his depiction of it, implies this envisioning of one's own freedom; at the same time, Joan's capacity for heroic action translates into a potential for creative enactment of that freedom. "She's got the creating mouth as well as the seeing eye," de Conte puts it, the "essential thing" enabling her to turn belief into fact (1:129). The key to her own creative independence, however, recalls her struggle with her voices, a struggle triggering a free flow of ideas. The thinking itself points to her great independence, and giving in to the compulsion of her voices is therefore an image of James's idea of the necessity to sacrifice the minor inner concerns to the major impelling drive after all becomes clear. This not only authenticates her independence but her actions as well. Joan's submission to the voices constitutes an embodiment and not an avoidance of authentic action and independent thinking.

This is the truth or experience that both Twain and James, as pragmatists, wished to fund. For James, such saintly models are "like the single drops which sparkle in the sun as they are flung far ahead of the advancing edge of a wave-crest or of a flood," glistening "forerunners" showing the way. Aligning their "creative energies" within an even more potent figure, James described "genuine saints" as "impregnators of the world, vivifiers and animators of potentialities" that "would lie forever dormant" but for their realization of these latent powers (*Varieties,* 325). For Twain, Joan's life dramatizes those vital forces lying latent within each individual, those rarely used but quite "usable and effective" powers, as he put it, those untried capacities for creative and independent thought.[41] Twain's text as a whole works to trigger this thought first of all through its ironical treatment of authoritative truth. Twain's irony releases the facts back to us as possibilities rather than dogma. Second, his juggling of narrative control continues to shift perspectival horizons and thus allow for a wider frame of reference, one that underlines the contingency of truth itself. Finally, Twain's description of those spiritual experiences central to Joan and her literary function as an ideal personality argue for an independent center or axis of creativity within each person, his vehicle for a true idea of freedom.

41. Mark Twain, "Saint Joan of Arc," 154.

Twain found significance in Joan's voices through understanding them in terms of his developing psychology, an understanding of human experience working from the concept of a divided self and increasing toward the potential release of this centrally creative impulse, an essentially religious effort to free the divine within. Continuing this effort in *No. 44, The Mysterious Stranger,* Twain leads us further within, toward this potential realm of creativity. The liminal experience that had briefly held Huck within the white banks of a Mississippi River fog and that had compelled Joan to submit to the white light of divine inspiration becomes central to Twain's further exploration of consciousness in his last major work. The problem now becomes not so much one of enacting one's freedom, or even defining it, but of imagining a world in which that freedom can exist.

— 3 —

Figuring Freedom as a Variety of
Religious Experience

No. 44, The Mysterious Stranger

But I your poor servant have revealed you to yourself
and set you free.
 —Mark Twain, *No. 44, The Mysterious Stranger*

"*I* believe the pragmatic way of taking religion to be the
deeper way. It gives it body as well as soul, it makes it
claim, as everything real must claim, some characteristic realm of fact as its very own." So concludes William James in the
final pages of *Varieties,* his study devoted to the spiritual claims upon
reality. "What the more characteristically divine facts are, apart from
the actual inflow of energy in the faith-state and the prayer state, I
know not," James confesses, but that "they exist" is the "over-belief"
he risks nurturing in his own life:

> The whole drift of my education goes to persuade me that the
> world of our present consciousness is only one out of many
> worlds of consciousness that exist, and that those other worlds
> must contain experiences which have meaning for our life also;
> and that although in the main their experiences and those of this
> world keep discrete, yet the two become continuous at certain
> points, and higher energies filter in. (463)[1]

1. For James, an "overbelief" is a belief in which we find a larger purpose in
our lives or through which we direct the feeling of being connected to some-

The point through which James believes the divine and mundane converge, or through which we encounter seemingly inexplicable facts, brings us to one of this chapter's principal concerns: Twain's fictional account of "other worlds" of consciousness.

Exploring those enigmatic relations that flourish within the darker interior of the self provides the central focus for reading *No. 44, The Mysterious Stranger,* Mark Twain's last and, in many ways, his most radical work. However, that radicality has often been denied due attention by a critical tendency to read it solely in terms of the grief and looming despair suffered by its author in his later years.

For James Cox, Twain's tale of August Feldner and his mysterious stranger reveals Twain as unable to "integrate and coordinate" his "dissipating" creative impulses during his final years. Arguing along the same lines, though reaching a different conclusion, Henry Nash Smith observes that from early on in his career, Twain had divided his literary voice between a "vernacular attitude" that spoke for an "actual world of experience" and a genteel view that spoke for a grander and more ideal realm of experience. Although Smith provides a stylistic analysis more than a philosophical one, he nonetheless reveals how Twain artistically maneuvered between ideal and mundane experience throughout much of his work. Smith concludes, however, that Twain ultimately rejected an apparently meaningless reality and found his repose in the spiritually transcendent voice that emerges in his tale of a mysterious stranger.[2]

Not allowing Twain even this amount of serious intent, Hamlin Hill simply dismisses *No. 44* as an artistic failure, little more than a "jumble of confused motives and ideas" revealing that old age had "dulled" and "crippled" Twain's imagination and "creative instincts." The work finds its rightful place, Hill believes, within that "junkyard of unfinished manuscripts and ill-conceived literary ideas" testifying to the "failure of Mark Twain to retain creative control over his world."[3] Admittedly, *No. 44* presents a critical challenge to anyone attempting to make sense of its often perplexing structure; however,

thing larger than ourselves. It centrally functions to give the self an active role within that grander scheme and usually includes the image of a divine force of some sort.

2. James Cox, *Mark Twain: The Fate of Humor,* 272, and Henry Nash Smith, *Mark Twain: The Development of a Writer,* 5, 186.

3. Hamlin Hill, *Mark Twain: God's Fool,* 113, 272–73.

to leap to the conclusion that it is a piece of literary junk or at best a meaningless tale of frustration is to engage in counterproductive critical foreclosure.

It is important to realize that *No. 44* has only recently come off the shelf. As one of three versions of a story Twain had worked on between 1897 and 1908, *No. 44* lay relatively unnoticed until 1963 and John S. Tuckey's study of the manuscripts. Tuckey was the first to call into serious question the traditional "authorized" editing of the manuscripts by Albert Bigelow Paine and F. A. Duneka, Twain's official biographer and literary publisher respectively. Both men had taken extraordinary liberties with Twain's work: repositioning passages and chapters, deleting and adding characters, and generally revising what they believed to be offensive. In spite of the heavy bowdlerizing, the 1916 Paine/Duneka text of *The Mysterious Stranger, A Romance* would remain canonical until Tuckey's challenge and the publication of the complete manuscripts by William Gibson in 1969. Although this cannot explain the lack of insight on the part of Hamlin Hill, it does help account for the critical blindness of Cox and Smith.

Bernard DeVoto had conducted his own intensive study of the drafts of Twain's tale, but was unable to publish his findings before his death. Tuckey acknowledges DeVoto in his own monograph, but points out that when DeVoto attempted to reconstruct the order in which the manuscripts were written, he misaligned the compositional dates around the accepted theory of a despairing Twain. DeVoto believed that the Paine/Duneka version was indeed Twain's final draft, one whose triumphant dream ending, which was actually the conclusion for *No. 44,* proved that by 1905, when Twain wrote "The Chronicle of Young Satan," he had conquered years of lingering doubt and confusion. For Tuckey, DeVoto's mistaken arrangement only furthered assumptions that Twain had been artistically impotent at least since the death of his favorite daughter Susy in 1896. By proving that Twain had been working on *No. 44* during this time, that it is a text neither lacking in talent nor creative energy, and that it was actually Twain's final manuscript, Tuckey called into question the reigning assumptions about Twain's final artistic endeavors.[4]

Therefore, with the publication of *Mark Twain's Mysterious Stranger Manuscripts,* Gibson not only exposed the nature and extent

4. See John S. Tuckey, *Mark Twain and Little Satan.*

of abusive editorializing, he also presented, along with Twain's working dates and notes, the three different manuscripts Twain developed over eleven years in their entirety: "The Chronicle of Young Satan," "Schoolhouse Hill," and "No. 44, The Mysterious Stranger." As Gibson points out, the Paine/Duneka publication consisted mainly of the first manuscript, "The Chronicle of Young Satan," which Twain began to write in 1897 and left unfinished in 1900. After tampering with what they believed to be its most derogatory passages, entirely deleting Twain's central portrait of a malicious priest, Paine and Duneka concluded their version of "Chronicle" by adding to it what, in actuality, is the final chapter of the manuscript "No. 44, The Mysterious Stranger."[5]

Twain began to work on the only version of *No. 44* that had clear ending in 1902. By 1904, Twain had completed 25 of 34 chapters, including the final one.[6] This concluding chapter has been the most perplexing of all for critics as it recast the entire tale as an interior narrative of the mind of the protagonist August Feldner, so that the entire narrative, at the end, must be rethought as a pilgrimage through multiple layers of the narrator's consciousness. This interior narrative is the tale Twain had been attempting to tell one way or another since 1897 (if not for most of his life); he finally succeeded in 1908, when he finished his work on *No. 44,* two years before his death. Although the story line within the novel can be as confusing as the history of its creation, often exhibiting labyrinthine twists and turns of its narrative consciousness, it nonetheless reveals that Twain's creative power was far from fading during the writing of his last major work.

Twain's power reached its peak in this tale of an almost unwittingly self-exploring mind, one that by leading us into and through the interior life of its protagonist fictionally opens James's other worlds of experience. *No. 44* brings to fruition Twain's complex ideas on the self and is the climax of his lifelong struggle with the problem of human freedom in the face of apparent necessity. In resolving his conflict about the nature of free and conditioned being, Twain turned to an extremely unorthodox religious conception of human nature, one positing the divided self as the necessary condition for a godlike,

5. William Gibson, *Mark Twain's Mysterious Stranger Manuscripts,* 2–3.
6. Ibid., 3–4.

creative freedom. Again William James helps us to understand this radical move, one that locates both Twain and James within what might now be considered as a religio-pragmatic perspective.

By the completion of *No. 44*, all of James's major works were available to Twain, and Twain's marks and comments in his own copy of the *Varieties* reveal that Twain took a special interest in James's theory of the divided self. James's theory, however, expands on his previous notions of a hidden or subliminal self, a level of thought outside ordinary margins of experience, and Twain's *No. 44* can be read as a fictional model incorporating the manifestations of this Jamesian subliminal self and its capabilities. In his story of a mysterious stranger, moreover, Twain fictionally accounts for the interactive play of discrete states of mind as a variety of religious experience. This interaction between differing worlds provides both the *Varieties* and *No. 44* with their central aporias and their conceptual breakthroughs.

Our first critical exercise must be to locate Twain and James within their study of psychic phenomena in general and the manifestations of subliminal activity in particular. Their interest in the paranormal cannot be separated from their developing psychologies and provides a foundation for the further linking of their descriptions of extraordinary mental states in *No. 44* and the *Varieties*. In Twain's copy of the *Varieties,* we see how he recognized the validity of James's particular analysis of various levels of consciousness within the purview of religious experience. After that, it is possible to examine the text of *No. 44* against James's masterwork. Through making these connections, we begin to see that with *No. 44, The Mysterious Stranger,* Twain provides us with a textual capstone to his ongoing search into the nature of the self and with a means for participating in a creative process of discovery and negotiation within that nature.

James, Twain, and the Exploration of Mental Frontiers

"Ever since the English Society for Psychical Research began its investigations," Twain wrote in 1891, "I have read their pamphlets with avidity."[7] Formed in 1882 to document and systematically investigate extraordinary manifestations of mental power, the S.P.R. represented an impressive group of researchers, including Henry and

---

7. Twain's statement can be found in his essay "Mental Telegraphy," 110.

Eleanor Sidgwick, Edmund Gurney, and Frederick W. H. Myers, as well as Mark Twain and William James. James lightheartedly called the society a "sort of weather bureau" for the accumulation of extrasensory reports.[8] However, with the rest of his colleagues in psychical research, James seriously sought to evaluate a range of psychic phenomena while, at the same time, defend the S.P.R. against the attacks of those scientific materialists who refused to admit paranormal research as a proper subject for either scientific or philosophic inquiry.

In her brief but useful discussion of the effect of the S.P.R. on the thinking of both Twain and James, Susan Gillman points out that even Charles Sanders Peirce, one of James's closest friends, critically attacked notable members of the S.P.R. for their lack of scientific discipline and dismissed what they considered their best research and most important findings as little more than a collection of unsubstantiated speculations. G. Stanley Hall, a one-time student of James's and notable American psychologist, went as far as to equate psychical researchers with superstitious savages, troglodytes that were out of time and place.[9] James redressed such critical treatment, however, by pointing out that scientific assumptions, themselves, held no absolute claims on eternal veracity. Furthermore, neither James nor Twain naively embraced every crackpot idea or fashionable theory nor did they willingly participate in superstitious savagery.

Like James, Twain attempted to keep his own private psychical research and speculations within the realm of "experimental" psychology. Alternating between belief and skepticism or, as Gibson notes, between "a rational and satiric view and a speculative and psychological view," Twain cast a particularly wary eye on the claims of mediums to have had communication with the dead, and especially those scenarios involving spiritual manifestations.[10] In "Schoolhouse Hill," the shortest version of Twain's tale in which Huck Finn and Tom Sawyer appear with an equally boyish but nameless and mysterious stranger, Twain's skepticism erupts in a burlesque of séances and mediums as his impish stranger fakes a

8. William James, "What Psychical Research Has Accomplished," 30.
9. Susan Gillman, *Dark Twins: Imposture and Identity in Mark Twain's America,* 141.
10. Gibson, *Manuscripts,* 27.

return from the dead of such dignitaries as Napoléon, Shakespeare, and Lord Byron (the latter's poetry suffering since "his mind had decayed" somewhat in the grave).[11]

Setting aside "The Chronicle of Young Satan," Twain worked on "Schoolhouse Hill" in November and December of 1898. In some ways this fragment provides a bridge from the dark cynicism of "Chronicle" to the dark laughter found in *No. 44*. Retaining his relations with Satan, now as his son instead of his nephew as in "Chronicle," Twain's protagonist now adopts the name of "44." Junior Satan/44 romps through St. Petersburg, astounding its inhabitants with his miraculous powers and comically deflating the shams and weak pretensions of ignorant villagers. His attempts to enlighten St. Petersburg appear to fail, however, as Twain's manuscript ends with the angelic stranger making plans for a further study of the human condition. "The fundamental change wrought in man's nature by my father's conduct must remain," he explains in the penultimate chapter, "but a part of its burden of evil consequences can be lifted," and "I will undertake it" by "ameliorating the condition of the race in some ways in *this* life."[12]

Like his evolving stranger, Twain had been working to improve the human condition by deflating the claims of spiritualists ever since his early journalistic writings; even as late as his "Mysterious Stranger Manuscripts," he felt it necessary to continue his subversion of spiritualistic frauds. However, as Howard Kerr correctly points out, Twain's satire was countered by a flickering hope that something real lay beyond the visible. Twain's actions outside his work demonstrated a similarly divided mind; his attempts to contact his daughter Susy after her death, upon the recommendation of Frederick Myers, reveal both an emotional need for a certain comfort and an intellectual need for creative expansion.[13] Indeed, Twain's comical treatment of séances in "Schoolhouse Hill" may have been as much a self-parodying act as an attack on the credibility of spiritualists, for his failed attempts to contact Susy through the use of a medium would have still been on his mind.

11. Mark Twain, "Schoolhouse Hill," 206.
12. Ibid., 217.
13. Howard Kerr, *Mediums, and Spirit-Rappers, and Roaring Radicals: Spiritualism in American Literature, 1850–1900*, 187.

If the dead could not be summoned, however, Twain nonetheless continued to believe that within the natural realm certain manifestations of mental power were still to be examined and understood. Again, much like James, who in the 1890s spoke and wrote about the subject of telepathy, as well as other psychic phenomena, Twain published his personal observations on the subject in two essays, "Mental Telegraphy" (1891), and "Mental Telegraphy Again" (1895). Twain had coined his own term for the phenomenon of thought transference a few years before the widely accepted term "telepathy" was introduced. In both of his essays he offered the corroborating testimonies of readers and acquaintances along with his personal experience of telepathic occurrences.

In particular, Twain recounted his own experiences with what he perceived to be the more common forms of telepathic communication, the crossing of letters in the mail or the foreknowledge of someone's visit or appearance before us. Twain recounted that one of the more striking examples of his telepathic powers occurred while visiting Washington, D.C., when the "spirit of prophecy" came upon him while in a local business. "Now I will go out this door," Twain recalls an inner voice directing him, "turn to the left, walk ten steps, and meet Mr. O_____ face to face." The meeting occurred exactly as Twain thought it would; because he knew the events "*beforehand*," this was another example, he believed, of a sort of telepathic communication. Twain's claimed ability to divine the content of letters before opening them was even more striking and may have set him apart, at least for himself, from those who possessed other forms of telepathy.[14] His experiences may be added to a "score" of similar ones mentioned by James in his essay "Telepathy," however, where James states that "if more and more of this solitary kind of evidence should accumulate, it would probably end by convincing the world."[15]

The point here is not to argue whether or not psychical phenomena exist, but to emphasize the importance of the subject in the thinking of Twain and James, especially during the last two decades of their lives. While wavering between belief and doubt, both men

14. Twain, "Mental Telegraphy," 99–101. Both "Mental Telegraphy" and "Mental Telegraphy Again" can be found in *The Science Fiction of Mark Twain*.
15. William James, "Telepathy," *Essays in Psychical Research*, 124–25.

would continue their investigations, out of curiosity and, perhaps, a spiritual need to experience such "forces . . . that bring redemption," forces that, according to James, are acknowledged by both psychology and religion as "seemingly outside of the conscious individual."[16] Both Twain and James, however, would remain primarily within the borders of experimental psychology, centering their search within the demonstrable parameters of human personality.

Tuckey points out that in December 1896 Twain was reading *Phantasms of the Living,* a two-volume study representing a vast collection of "supernormal" experiences as recorded by members of the S.P.R.[17] Written by Edmund Gurney, Frederick Myers, and Frank Podmore, *Phantasms* provided a collection of the proceedings of the Society for Psychical Research, covering such topics as telepathy, apparitions, dream experiences, and clairvoyance. Moreover, Twain had already read and marked the margins of his copy of *The Principles of Psychology,* in which James devoted a fair number of pages to altered states of being. Like James and other psychic explorers, Twain was developing his own perspective on alternate states of consciousness, especially in relation to such phenomena as dreams, hypnotism, and multiple personalities, which James also termed divided selves. In fact, Twain specifically mentioned James's investigations into psychical phenomena, along with those of certain French investigators, in his unpublished version of "My Platonic Sweetheart" (1898). Such citations support the validity of his speculations about the dream self and its autonomous existence in this brief story about his ongoing and innocent dream relationship with a seventeen-year-old sweetheart.[18] Earlier, in an 1897 notebook entry, Twain discussed at some length this "seeming *duality"* (Twain's emphasis), this apparent "presence in us of another person," as a "haunting mystery." This

16. James, *Varieties,* 196.

17. Tuckey, *Twain and Little Satan,* 26–27. Twain mistakenly refers to the text as "Apparitions of the Living" in his own notes (Typescript p. 36, Mark Twain Papers), but Gribben correctly lists *Phantasms of the Living* in *Mark Twain's Library,* 2:282.

18. Mark Twain's abridged version of "My Platonic Sweetheart" was published posthumously in the December 1912 issue of *Harper's.* My reference here is to the unpublished manuscript and typescript, both of which can be found in the Mark Twain Papers, Bancroft Library, University of California, Berkeley, No. 3A (Manuscript) and No. 3B (Typescript), Box 16.

presence would attract his attention throughout his final years of writing. The rest of this particular entry, dated January 7, 1898, is given over to a hypothetical construction of different levels of consciousness as Twain attempts to account for a waking and more spiritualized dreaming self.[19] Although more must be said of his speculations as we engage in a closer examination of Twain's *No. 44*, what is important here is that from the beginnings of his work on the "Mysterious Stranger Manuscripts" (1897), Twain left strong evidence of his deep and continuing interest in the paranormal theorizing of William James.

Oddly enough, James's *Psychology* would not have provided Twain with a dream theory as such. Unlike Freud, who revolutionized psychology with his publication of *The Interpretation of Dreams*, James never systematically developed a method for decoding or determining the meaning of dreams. Freud, himself, would become another notable member of the S.P.R. in 1911, but his primarily clinical approach to paranormal phenomena separated him from Twain and James who, like their nineteenth-century colleagues, were more open to the reality of intuitive understanding or what James simply refers to in *Varieties* as "something" beyond physical or psychical origins. It is worth emphasizing this difference here in a little more detail, because this difference points toward the religious and pragmatist thought informing the psychology of both Twain and James.

There is no record that either Twain or James read Freud's work on dream interpretation; no English translation was available until 1909, the year before the deaths of both Twain and James. James, however, had read Freud's and Breuer's 1893 article "On the Psychical Mechanism of Hysterical Phenomenon" in its original German. Briefly commenting upon it in a one-page review, after devoting four pages to a review of Pierre Janet's *"L'état Mental des Hystériques,"* James emphasized the essay's confirmation of Janet's idea of the hysteric's split consciousness but chose to ignore the article's other significant claim about the determining factors associated with the divided mind and the subconscious.[20]

---

19. Twain, *Notebook*, 348–50. Paine mistakenly records the date at the head of this entry as "London, Jan. 7, '97."

20. See Nathan Hale's *Freud and the Americans: The Beginning of Psychoanalysis in the United States, 1876–1917*, 128, 183.

Such a selective assessment is somewhat understandable, since neither Twain nor James would ever look upon the subconscious as a storehouse of determining behavioral factors. Indeed, both men were more aligned with the thinking of Janet and Alfred Binet, who felt that we might fruitfully cultivate unusual mental powers; in *Psychology,* James particularly discussed the importance of their findings concerning a "secondary consciousness" (1:203). For his own part, as noted in an 1897 notebook entry, Twain would accept the findings of the French psychologists as echoing his own concerning dreams and the useful effects of a divided self.

James finally met Freud, however, at the 1909 Clark University conference in Worcester, Massachusetts. An eclectic group of American intellectuals had gathered at Clark to welcome Freud during his only visit to the United States and to hear a series of lectures he was to deliver on the subject of psychoanalysis. James came away puzzled and suspicious; as he explained in a letter to Theodore Flournoy, he personally rejected Freud's "symbolism" as a "dangerous method" for determining the meaning of dreams. Yet he remained characteristically hopeful. Although he found Freud's "dream theories" incomprehensible and Freud himself "a man obsessed with fixed ideas," as he wrote to Flournoy, he hoped that "Freud and his pupils [would] push their ideas to their utmost limits, so that we may learn what they are." In another letter to one of his former students, Mary Calkins, James conceded that Freud's ideas may yet be useful though he suspected Freud himself, "with his dream theory, of being a regular hallucine."[21]

More like Twain than Freud, James preferred to approach dreams as yet another expression of a potentially useful subliminal self. James had offered his own early speculations upon the subliminal or "buried self" in *Psychology,* recognizing that the "total possible consciousness may be split into parts which coexist but mutually ignore each other." However, the "dream-world" and, as he explained in a later chapter, the hidden self may erupt from the subliminal side of our existence and "is very apt to remain figuring in our consciousness as a sort of sub-universe alongside of the waking world" (1:209, 206;

21. James to Theodore Flournoy, September 28, 1909, in *The Letters of William James,* 2:327–28. James to Mary Calkins, September 19, 1909, in Perry's *The Thought and Character of William James,* 2:123.

2:294). For Twain and James, this subliminal world was more likely to be a path leading to spiritual power than one toward revealing, imposing, or governing dysfunctional mental or physical behavior.

Nathan Hale, in his study of American writers' relations with developing notions of the unconscious, explains that this attempt to empower the self spiritually within the convincing argument of scientific determinism separated American thinkers from Freud. It was "an important strain of American belief," a "faith in the ordinary man's inner light," that caused American writers to diverge from Freud and, for the most part, guided James and Twain in their psychical research. For Hale, this "survival of Transcendentalism" was best typified in William James, who in attempting to combine psychology and paranormal research succeeded in developing a type of religious psychology that involved mental (or even spiritual) therapeutics.[22]

James, in fact, defended the benefits of such a psychology and was particularly angry with Freud's condemnation of "American religious therapy," as James wrote to Flournoy; as for Freud's attack on the use of psychology for mental healing and spiritual enlightenment, James could only answer with "Bah!"[23] No doubt, this difference of opinion helps to explain, to some degree, James's reaction to Freud's lectures at the Clark University conference. However, long before meeting Freud or hearing his critique of a peculiarly American psychology, James defended mental therapeutics in *Varieties,* finding the "Mind-cure" movements of his time particularly effective in engaging the "spiritual in man" with the "modern psychology of the subliminal self" (97).

James nearly claimed as much in both the opening and concluding chapters of *Psychology,* where in the first chapter he labeled his philosophy as a "religion," agreeing with those who posit "intelligence" as the prime mover of the universe (8). In the last chapter, James explained that his own philosophy of experience allows for a certain transcendent cognitive relation, not necessarily supernatural but one in which a "particular sort of natural agency" may exist alongside "other more recondite natural agencies" (625). His efforts to present psychology itself as a natural science, so as to lend some credibility to a developing discipline, may explain his relative neglect

22. Hale, *Freud and the Americans,* 228–29.
23. James to Flournoy, September 28, 1909, 328.

of the study of dreams and other psychical phenomena in his first major work.

With his description of the fringe relations that accompany one's stream of consciousness, James opened the way in his *Psychology* for future investigations into vaguely perceived regions of mind. At the same time, in his discussions of experimental fields of study in *Psychology,* including hypnotism, hallucinations, or unusual mental states, James suggested that the material reality on which science builds may be only one of several realities.[24] Finding in "sleep and dreaming" the "true analogues of the hypnotic trance," James suggested that hypnotism, like dreams, argues convincingly for a "double consciousness" and may be a useful tool for eliciting the actions of secondary selves (2:600).

For James, as well as for Twain, another reality might well hold in other levels of the self, in what James's contemporary Frederick Myers was the first to call the "subliminal self." In his introduction to *Human Personality and Its Survival of Bodily Death,* Myers separated subliminal from supraliminal thought by defining the former as lying beneath the ordinary threshold of consciousness and the latter as ordinary consciousness. For Myers, evolutionary changes collected and continued to bury within the mind all that was once "vividly present," though prior experience could spring forth at different times into what he called a "subliminal uprush," an eruption of latent knowledge through the threshold of consciousness.[25] Dreams, hypnotism, and altering personalities were instances of the overflow of such a subliminal stream, though both Myers and James believed the spring of subliminal thought could be tapped in other ways, especially in instances of genius.

In James's opinion, Twain provided such an instance of genius. In his 1896 "Lowell Lectures on Exceptional Mental States," which have only recently been painstakingly reconstructed by Eugene Taylor, James specifically mentioned Mark Twain, along with such other

24. See especially the chapters "The Stream of Thought," "The Consciousness of Self," and "Hypnotism."

25. Frederick W. H. Myers, *Human Personality and Its Survival of Bodily Death,* 71. This posthumous collection of Myers's articles, all written during the 1890s, focuses upon those phenomena that for Myers represent incursions from subliminal regions of the self, eruptions of "thoughts" and "feelings" outside the margins of "ordinary" consciousness (71–72).

luminaries as Emerson, Thoreau, Margaret Fuller, Kipling, Saint Paul, and Sarah Bernhardt, in his lecture titled "Genius." For James, such genius represents "first class originality of intellect," not just a psychopathology of the artist as a few were beginning to suggest. Attempting to alert the medical profession, in particular, to the importance of all such matters, James defended and welcomed the "sensibilities, impulses, and obsessions" attributed to genius, as well as to dreams, multiple personalities, and even demonic possession; such extraordinary phenomena deepen the "field of our experience," James pointed out, and add all "the better" to the store of human understanding.[26] James would argue his case in more depth in the *Varieties,* where he eventually added Tolstoy and Bunyan to his list of geniuses, whom he defended as those persons in which a "superior intellect and psychopathic temperament" may indeed "coalesce," the former being effectively released by the latter. Also, the "psychopathic temperament," James explained, offers that "emotionality" and "intensity" that are essential not only to "effective genius" but also to affective religious experience as well (29–30). James thus linked both intellectual genius and religious experience to a particular personality that is open to multiple impulses and an unusual degree of subliminal thought.

James therefore agreed with Myers, as the lecture notes reveal, that superior thinking can be explained "in truth" as "a subliminal uprush" and as the "power of appropriating the results of subliminal mentation to subserve the supraliminal stream of thought."[27] The resultant thoughts, as James continued in his notes, define both the subliminal and the genius:

> But turn to the highest order of minds . . . [where] we have the most abrupt cross cuts and transitions from one idea to another . . . the most unheard of combinations of elements . . . [where] we seem suddenly introduced into a seething cauldron of ideas, where everything is fizzling and bobbing about in a state of bewil-

26. Eugene Taylor, *William James on Exceptional Mental States: The 1896 Lowell Lectures,* 159–60, 164. Eugene Taylor reconstructed the Lowell lectures, which read like a primer to James's *Varieties,* through an examination of James's notes, correspondence, and marginalia.
27. Ibid., 149.

dering activity, where partnerships can be loosened or joined in an instant . . . and the unexpected seems the only law.[28]

Reaffirming an essentially romantic view, James then cited the channeling of this spontaneous rush of thought into creative activity as genius in action.

As a genius particularly responsive to the "seething cauldron of ideas," Twain found the expression of these ideas increasingly difficult during his later years. *No. 44*, then, can be read not only as a fictional model incorporating the manifestations of the subliminal self and its capabilities but as Twain's attempt to fashion a coherent presentation of his own capabilities, to mirror the workings of his own inner life. However, before approaching such intimate disclosures, we need to turn to Twain's own copy of James's *The Varieties of Religious Experience: A Study in Human Nature*. Although Twain's notations and comments on the *Varieties* run only through the chapter on "The Sick Soul," approximately a third of the book, they suffice to illuminate the mind of one of James's most important readers, the one who created August Feldner's often baffling encounter with his mysterious stranger.

Twain as Armchair Editor of James

In his copy of the *Varieties*, Twain entered various marks, underlinings, and comments on the opening chapter, "Religion and Neurology." Twain wrote "motto for my book" next to James's inclusion of Spinoza's declaration of philosophical intent "'I will analyze the actions and appetites of men as if it were a question of lines, of planes, and of solids.'" James then paraphrased Spinoza, who intended to "consider our passions and their properties with the same eye with which he looks on all other natural things," with an eye toward natural causes. A few lines below, Twain wrote "another" next to James's inclusion of Hippolyte Taine's remark that the origins of all human experience, "'whether the facts be moral or physical'" ought to be studied (17, 18).[29] Twain made check marks beside

28. Ibid., 160.
29. As mentioned before, Twain's copy of the *Varieties* is owned by Judge Harry Pregerson. To avoid confusion, however, all page numbers given here refer to my own working text of James's *Varieties*.

James's recognition that while such statements as Spinoza's and Taine's may seem to threaten "our soul's vital secrets," the knowledge of the soul's mystery should in no way diminish its significance in human experience (*Varieties,* 18). The primary reason we value experiences at all is not because we can trace their original antecedents, according to James, but because we find them pleasurable or "we believe them to bring us good consequential fruits for life" (22). It is from this pragmatic perspective, a view focusing on a useful verification of religious claims instead of a deadening denial of the same, that James began his own study of spiritual experiences. James attempted not so much to divide and classify and, in the process, nullify their religious or psychical worth, but to discover what "insight into truth" or what "wider scope" of human experience might be encountered through them. James concluded his opening chapter upon this intent, which Twain marked with a double line in the margin.

In James's chapter "The Religion of Healthy-Mindedness," which Twain marked with a few wavy lines, James borrowed an old distinction from Francis W. Newman to separate individuals into two primary types: the "once-born" and the "twice-born" (79). These types are important for James's discussion of the sick soul in the following chapter, and a brief examination of James's description of them will help us assess Twain's later and more thorough markings of that chapter.

The "once-born," with souls of a "sky-blue tint and believing happiness to be the only criteria of religion's truth," as James suspects in the *Varieties,* exhibit a "temperament organically weighted on the side of cheer" and an "optimism" seemingly "quasi-pathological" (79, 81–82). Citing Whitman and Emerson as primary examples of once-born optimism, representatives of those "men who seem to have started in life with a bottle or two of champagne inscribed to their credit" (128), James holds them up as well as purveyors of a "systematic cultivation of healthy-mindedness as a religious attitude," one that reflects, to a large degree, the survival instinct within us all:

> We divert our attention from disease and death as much as we can; and the slaughterhouses and indecencies without end on which our life is founded are huddled out of sight and never mentioned, so that the world we recognize officially in literature and in society is a poetic fiction far handsomer and cleaner and better than the world that really is. (88)

James selectively quoted Whitman (ignoring the realism found, say, in "Drum Taps") and pinpointed the central motivation of the healthy-minded individual, a motivation that, for James, may be called a religious attitude, a purposeful "reaction on the whole nature of things" that "loyally binds [one] to certain inner ideals" (89). Although Whitman and Emerson never purported to be purveyors of religion, James saw them as forerunners, if not prophets, of the religious movements flowering in turn-of-the-century America, in particular, "Mind Cure" or "Christian Science" (91–93).

Twain had an ambivalent relationship with both movements and wrote at length on the Christian Science movement and its founder, Mary Baker Eddy. In his 1907 book *Christian Science,* which Twain introduced as an attempt to characterize Mrs. Eddy and the "nature and scope of her Monarchy," he firmly professed his faith in mental healing, "The power which a man's imagination has over his body to heal it or make it sick is a force which none of us is born without."[30] However, many of us live without realizing our mental capabilities until a forceful provocateur awakens our imaginative potential. "From the beginning of time the sorcerer, the interpreter of dreams, the fortune-teller, the charlatan, the quack, the wild-man, the educated physician, the mesmerist, and the hypnotist" have known about the mind's power over bodily ailments, as Twain observes, and they "have made use of the client's *imagination* to help them in their work."[31] Twain has no argument, then, with mental healing as such, but nonetheless questions the intentions of its practitioners and the nature of their "work," singling out Mary Baker Eddy and her motivations as particularly questionable and worthy of comic disposition.

In *No. 44,* Twain attacks the story's founder of what he dubs "Christian Silence," for the "uninterpretable irrelevancies" of her

30. Mark Twain, *Christian Science,* 84. Between 1898 and 1899, Twain wrote most of the first book to *Christian Science.* Putting the manuscript aside for a few years, he finished the second book, which vehemently denounces Eddy and "Eddy-worship," in 1903. In *The Secret History of Eddypus, the World Empire,* a much shorter diatribe against Christian Science, Twain envisioned a bleak and morally regressive future overshadowed by Eddy's monarchy.

31. Twain, *Christian Science,* 34. Twain concluded *Christian Science* by locating Eddy somewhere between a charlatan and a wild quack. In claiming access to the "inpouring of the Spirit of God" (271), Eddy demanded far too much from Twain's faith.

"incomprehensible and uninterpretable" teachings (166). In one of the story's more hilarious moments, Twain transforms a lady-in-waiting into a chatty cat. By providing the cat with the portmanteau name Mary Florence Fortescue Baker G. Nightingale, Twain converges Florence Nightingale's dedication to the relief of suffering humanity into what he saw as Mary Baker Eddy's imposition of suffering through her opaque teachings (157). After suffering through the talkative cat's inability to distinguish the literal from the metaphorical, as Twain illustrated the intellectual limits of the founder of Christian Science and her catlike slyness, Twain's narrator finally silences the animal by warning that "if you open your mouth again I'll jam the bootjack down it! you're as random and irrelevant and incoherent and mentally impenetrable as the afflicted Founder herself" (176). Silenced, the cat finds safety under the bed, "reflecting, probably, if she had the machinery for it" (176).

Twain's attack is best read as directed at Eddy's exercise of personal power rather than at the mind-cure movement of Christian Science. As Justin Kaplan reminds us in his biographical assessment of Twain's later years, Twain often championed the efficacy of "mind-cure," permitting both himself and his daughters to undergo the treatments of mind-curists, as did many of his friends such as the Howellses and William James.[32] Through the urgings of Elinor Howells and James, in fact, Twain had come to accept the whole field of mental healing as essentially a form of hypnotism.[33] Perhaps to some degree, as Kaplan suggests, Twain was engaging in such mental therapeutics as an escape from the personal and financial pressures darkening his later years. However, his temperament would never allow him to escape pragmatics for long or to completely accept the unyielding optimism of mind-cure movements. In James's terms, Twain belonged within the camp of the "twice-born."

Twain's markings suggest that he found the chapter "The Sick Soul" particularly engaging; in this chapter, James turns toward an analysis of the twice born, those who shoulder the "burden of the consciousness of evil" yet find it no "stumbling block" or "terror." They work through their own "prison-house" of "consciousness" and on into a "second birth, a deeper" and far superior "kind of conscious

32. Justin Kaplan, *Mr. Clemens and Mark Twain*, 385.
33. Ibid.

being" (126, 128, 146). James uses Tolstoy and Bunyan as his primary examples, though he may well have been thinking of Twain, since the "pathological melancholy" he attributes to Tolstoy is descriptive of Twain's own bouts of depression. Moreover, when James defended Twain and Tolstoy in his "Lowell Lectures on Exceptional Mental States"—he described both as artistic geniuses whose "psychopathic peculiarities" or "morbid" temperaments serve to pluralize experience—we can partially link the two psychologically (163–65). Again, quoting from *My Confession,* James interprets Tolstoy's "desire to get rid of my existence" and "out of life" as not only the effect of disillusionment but also a reflection of a "fearful melancholy self-contempt and despair" (147), attitudes and feelings epitomized in much of Twain's later writings, especially in "What Is Man?"

Twain also revealed his sense of affinity with the melancholic Tolstoy through his annotations beside James's analysis of Tolstoy's personality; they suggest an attempt to use Tolstoy in order to identify and understand his own troubled mind. At the same time, Twain took especial note of James's quotations of lesser-known suffering melancholics. Twain's marks begin near James's inclusion of the recollections of Father Gratry; Twain placed a check next to Gratry's confession of his own sense of damnation (137). Next to a particularly bleak letter from an anonymous asylum patient, who bemoaned his "misfortune" of birth into the "bitterness" of life, Twain scribbled a few wavy lines, and drew a few similar marks next to Tolstoy's disenchanted view of life as a "stupid jest" or as a "stupid cheat." He more emphatically bracketed Tolstoy's conclusion that the "meaningless absurdity of life" must be the "only incontestable knowledge accessible to man" (145). Twain's growing disillusionment during his later years has been elsewhere documented, and his notations here seem to confirm a self-analytical concern with his darker moods.[34]

However, critics have failed to fully consider the religious significance of Twain's changing moods, and though his disillusionment is similar to Tolstoy's general despair of universal purpose, it is even more like what James described as the sort of "religious melancholy" found in John Bunyan's autobiography. James described Bunyan as

34. Van Wyck Brooks's *The Ordeal of Mark Twain* and Hamlin Hill's *Mark Twain: God's Fool,* of course, still provide two of the more insightful psycho/biographical studies of Twain's later years.

"sensitive of conscience to a diseased degree" and as constantly "beset by doubts" about himself and the human race in general; Bunyan feared that both were damned (147). Twain's similar doubts about human goodness surface within most of his major works and perhaps reach the point of despair in his creation of "Hadleyburg," a community whose complete corruption is exposed by one of Twain's earlier mysterious strangers.

Twain also exposes the darker side of his own nature in "The Facts Concerning the Recent Carnival of Crime in Connecticut," as he struggled with his own tortured conscience for control of his thoughts and actions. Twain, in fact, acknowledged his "Carnival of Crime" as the first in a series of investigations into the divided self. "I made my conscience that other person," he records in his note-book, "and it came before me in the form of a malignant dwarf and told me plain things about myself and shamed me and scoffed at me and derided me."[35] However, his own early portrayal of con-science, as Twain recorded in a notebook entry about Robert Louis Stevenson's in the tale of Jekyll and Hyde, failed to account for the completely separate existence of the self's double. Working from his own readings of investigations into the phenomenon of multiple personalities, Twain eventually decided that the "two persons in a man do not even know each other . . . have never even suspected each other's existence."[36]

Twain's continuing speculations upon this other within, this sec-ond self that often exposes dark mental meanderings, undoubtedly reveals his more dismal moods and may be said to "carry him a little farther over the misery-threshold" and on toward that experience of "world-sickness" that, for James, typifies the melancholic's darkest moment (*Varieties,* 131). James described his own momentous attack of religious melancholy in *Varieties* with a dreadful image of another self, one that came to him suddenly in one of his earlier states of "philosophic pessimism." James explains how he, while thus depressed, had an overpowering image of an epileptic patient, who was passively idiotic and perceptually vacant as well, that filled his mind with a mirror of the precariousness of his own mental state. Realizing the thin line between mental health and helpless idiocy,

35. Paine, *Notebook,* 348.
36. Ibid., 349–50.

James broke down in a "mass of quivering fear . . . a horrible dread at the pit of [his] stomach . . . and with a sense of the insecurity of life" (149). Although James finally lifted himself from this "pit of insecurity," primarily through his choice to believe in the efficacy of his actions, he would always remain sympathetically united with the "morbid feelings of others" (*Varieties,* 150).[37]

In his collection of James's letters, James's son Henry attributes his father's "religious despondency" to his constant reflections upon the "problem of the moral constitution of things," questions about "man's relation to the Universe" and whether such a relation be "significant or impotent and meaningless." These questions fell like an oppressive burden upon the mental shoulders of William James.[38] At such times, James must have wanted the same release from those burdensome thoughts as Twain implicitly yearned for in the last comment to be found in his copy of James's *Varieties.* After an evangelist describes the weight of a lifetime of sin and guilt and his resulting envy of the beasts who have no concept of damnation, James explains that such envy "seems to be a very wide-spread affection in this type of sadness" (148–49); below which, Twain writes, "I had it." Twain's "envy," moreover, much like James's fear of mental fragmentation, reveals a wish for nonexistence, a desire to simply vanish. The experience is also like Bunyan's, as James further explains, and exemplifies the "high-water mark" of religious melancholy (148).

James considered his own ultimate "experience of melancholy" to have "had a religious bearing" as well, one that for sanity's sake compelled him to seek spiritual refuge in extramarginal regions of the self. In much the same way, Twain's despondent recognition of his envy led him to a similar refuge in his art, imagination, and creative soul. It is from that creative space that Twain figured forth August Feldner's encounter with the mysterious 44, a meeting between distinct parts of mind that proves to be complex and confusing—though not entirely bleak.

37. While James recorded this melancholic experience in the *Varieties* as the testimony of an anonymous "correspondent," his son Henry verifies the experience as his father's own in his collection of *The Letters of William James,* 1:145.
38. Ibid.

Telling the Tale of a Mysterious Stranger

Twain sets his tale in Austria in the year 1490. Setting his tale only two years before Columbus's arrival in the New World, Twain may here be making a connection to his attempt to figure forth a new vision of freedom. Along similar lines, his narrator the Sieur Louis de Conte begins recording his recollections of Joan of Arc in 1492. The setting certainly recalls the blissful appearance of the St. Petersburg of Huck Finn or the Domremy of Joan of Arc:

> Yes, Austria was far from the world, and asleep, and our village was in the middle of that sleep, being in the middle of Austria. It drowsed in peace where the news from the world hardly ever came to disturb its dreams, and was infinitely content. At its front flowed the tranquil river, its surface painted with cloud-forms . . . behind it rose the woody steeps to the base of the lofty precipice; from the top of the precipice frowned the vast castle of Rosenfeld. (*No. 44*, 3–4)

Twain's opening image seems to invite us to dream, or into a dream, or into a time and place fabricated upon dreams, while at the same time it prefigures his final chapter, which denies any ultimate distinction between the waking and dreaming world. In that same final chapter, we learn that the entire tale of the mysterious stranger has in fact been an interior dream of Twain's narrator August Feldner, whose narrative has been a dream of a life within a dream.

Twain provides a similar revelation in his earlier *A Connecticut Yankee in King Arthur's Court* (1889), a tale framed within the multiple layers of a dreaming self: one shared by author and narrator. The initial meeting between the author's persona and the Yankee Hank Morgan occurs between and within the dreams of one another as the tale slips into the imaginative space of Arthurian England. All is not well in this textual dreamscape, however, and Twain's depiction of the cruelty and ignorance undergirding the Victorian myth of Camelot soon becomes the story's primary focus. By tale's end, facing the apparent cosmic cruelty of death, we find Morgan drifting in a liminal space between real and imagined worlds. "It was awful—awfuler than you could ever imagine," the Yankee concludes deliriously, "as real as reality" and as "strange" and "hideous."[39] For the Twain of

---

39. Mark Twain, *Connecticut Yankee*, 446–47.

Connecticut Yankee, and sporadically of his later dream tales, imagining a better reality seemed a doomed project. Past and present reality could only be read as the worst of all possible nightmares.

By no means does Twain ignore the horrors of existence or the claims of history in *No. 44,* where in a subtextual use of the concept of dreams, he sets in motion the conflicting hopes and dreams of a struggling humanity. Conflating the images of past and present within the playing field of human ignorance, he continues to denounce apparently timeless shams, the economic and political forces that would enslave body and mind. In *No. 44,* the institutional Church is personified as a drunken, lecherous, hypocritical priest, bent on extorting the wages of sin from fearful parishioners; union tyranny is clearly satirized in Twain's farcical creation of duplicate selves as scabs; and the imperialistic temper that Twain so loathed is attacked in both his ridicule of Mary Baker Eddy and his derision of the spoils of conquest in the penultimate chapter, "Assembly of the Dead."

Even the heavenly image that pervades Twain's opening setting fades upon closer inspection. The Austrian village of Eseldorf appears to be a paradise with its "little homesteads nested among orchards and shade trees," as August describes it, with its "mental and spiritual clock" still in the "Age of Faith" (3–4). Though this paradise belongs to Prince Rosenfeld, his castle, which looms over paradise, is unoccupied except for the servants who keep it up in expectation of their master's return. Knowing the German translation of Eseldorf to be "assville," we might interpret the castle's temporary tenants to be working and waiting like foolish asses within a paradise. We might also read the opening as an image of a class-structure with an absentee landlord and the folk left to shift as best as they can. Such a case could be made since the castle itself is to become a ground for the political and economic struggle of its inhabitants: power-seeking priests, magicians, and professional tradesmen.

However, as with Langland's image of the opening field of folk in *Piers Plowman,* these images can never escape their religious connotations, especially within the governing allusion of a paradisal setting. We might see the Eseldorfians as people either waiting for or upon God, as foolish asses maintaining the dwelling of a god who has abandoned them or already died, or else working through a purgatorial labor in the midst of a promised paradise, or awaiting the Lord's return.

Twain's opening images quite successfully resist the imposition of any one interpretive perspective. The economic and political thrust of these early images persists through the text as Twain almost seamlessly integrates the struggle between union and non-union workers into his portrayal of duplicate or dream selves. A religious interpretation is legitimized in the explicit contrast between the institutional Church and 44 himself, as well as in the latter's continual revelations of inward powers.[40] However, while Twain resisted a single interpretation, he still developed a unifying theme through the revelations of 44. He ended the tale by situating its action back within the purview of dreams or, more specifically, within the "visions" and "fictions" dreamed up by a race of asses (186).

What unites all the asses is their inability to create more sufficient fictions, to envision better economic, political, or spiritual conditions for themselves. In his concluding remarks, 44 rails at the absurdity of funding a stale and insane "reality," the very one his tale reveals, and he especially targets the perpetuation of a cruel God as the most vicious of all possible fictions (186–87). Twain's text indicts the imaginative failure and intellectual dependency of his culture even as it seeks to provide a means for freeing our thoughts and transforming our fictions into images more worthy of belief.

Forty-four outwits all attempts by others to control or contain his thought and action. Even in his position as a new apprentice within the print shop of Rosenfeld's castle, he quickly becomes the center of attraction and the focus of attention. He stands outside the rest of the "herd" (August's name for his fellow denizens of the castle) primarily because of his "indifference" to their opinion or authority. August is reluctant to befriend 44 because he is inhibited by his own fears of rejection; however, he nonetheless desires the freedom of movement and thought the stranger offers. He slowly finds that his own life has taken on a "fresh novelty" since 44's arrival in Eseldorf, and he "passionately longed to know" him better (28). August actually finds himself envying 44's unusual abilities, which had even rivaled those of the castle's magician. So "one night after the herd were in bed," as he recalls, he secretly "slipped up" to the

40. It is useful to remember, in this connection, that in his two earlier manuscripts, Twain gave 44 the name *Satan,* but here canceled that name.

stranger's room and waited by the door for his arrival. Well after midnight, 44 appeared.

This secretive meeting is strikingly similar to the one found in "My Platonic Sweetheart" and its description of "Dreamland" as a place where extraordinary phenomena are the reality. "My Platonic Sweetheart" can even be read as a companion piece to *No. 44*. Like the relationship that August and 44 come to share, Twain's own innocent affair with his dream "sweetheart" satisfies his soulful longings for spiritual contentment and creative freedom. Twain's shorter dream narrative also reveals his progress toward the solipsistic suggestion in *No. 44* that reality is a creature of our own thought. "We know" that the objects of our dreams truly exist, as Twain explains in his tale of platonic intimacy, "because there are no such things here, and they must be there, because there is no other place."[41] It is just a short imaginative leap to *No. 44* and the conclusion that reality itself originates in the "other place."

The leap of mind begins, however, in the initial encounter between 44 and August. Mental telepathy becomes the norm of communication as 44 acknowledges August's thoughts before hearing them; the stranger caters to the whims of his intimate companion serving up his first desire, "claret, blazing hot" (30). "I couldn't resist," August confesses; "it was nectar," and "I indulged myself" (30). However, August resists a complete acceptance of the stranger:

> He wanted me to sleep in his own bed, and said he didn't need it . . . but I shuddered at the idea, and got out of it by saying I should rest better in my own, because I was accustomed to it. So then he stepped outside the door with me . . . and I stepped feebly into the black gloom—and found myself in my own bed, with my door closed, [and] my candle blinking on the table . . . (31)

If this is "all a dream," as August concludes the following morning—though 44 continues to claim his own reality—then the narrator's first private encounter with his mysterious dream self finds August resisting that self's intrusive behavior, struggling against its suggestions, while at the same time tentatively indulging in its whims and fancies.

41. See the published version of "My Platonic Sweetheart," in *The Science Fiction of Mark Twain*, 125.

However, can it be that August indulges, however hesitantly, in his own fanciful flights? At this point, we require some analytic help; we will find what we need in James.

In his *Psychology,* James theorizes on just such a dream self or secondary selves as an explanation for the curious occurrences of divided or multiple personalities. When these selves meet within what James calls the "phenomenon of alternating personality," whether within a dream or a hypnotic trance, the secondary self often emerges as the superior of the two, setting up an inward tension (379–80). In the cases of "double or alternate personality," as James calls it, this superior self rises in opposition to the "dullness and melancholy" that he ascribes to the primary or waking self (384). The removal of these "inhibitions" (James's word for the dull or melancholic inclinations) comes only through the gradual impositions of the secondary character.

In the *Varieties,* James develops his theory of secondary selves further in his chapter "The Divided Self." He situates the inner tensions of struggling selves in what he calls the "heterogeneous" personality, one in which compelling ideas or "irrational impulses . . . dreads" and "inhibitions" tug at rational control. As James explains, hagiographies are complete with similar heterogeneous struggles, "inscribed invariably to the direct agency of Satan" (158). Although Twain keeps his stranger's identity a secret in his tale's final version, as we have noted in the earlier "Chronicle of Young Satan," it is an orator of Satan, if not the devil himself, who tempts the narrator out of his restrictive thought; while in the middle of the version "Schoolhouse Hill," one of Satan's sons struggles to make a persuasive case for the innocence of his father.[42] In refusing to make a similar identification in *No. 44,* Twain fictionally reiterates the point James continually argues in *Varieties,* that this phenomenon of experiencing visitations from within, even if the visitor appears to be Satan himself, "connects itself with the life of the subconscious, so-called," and "chiefly consist[s] in the straightening out of the inner self" (158).

This alignment of selves is just as important for Twain, and his

---

42. Gibson, *Manuscripts,* 165, 216. In "The Chronicle of Young Satan," Twain's young narrator ultimately realizes that his mind is changing beneath the "strong personality" of Satan, and in "Schoolhouse Hill," Satan's son convinces a gullible spiritualist of his father's good intentions.

removal of the demonic identification from 44 suggests that Twain, like James, was investigating the manifestations of subliminal thought or subconscious life. A closer look at the initial meeting between 44 and August reveals that Twain solidifies this particular connection through his forwarding imagery.

The suggestive invitations of 44 tempt August to cross an unknown mental threshold, from an "accustomed" bed to an "unaccustomed" one, and point to Twain's emphatic use of "doors" as the opening across that threshold. Doors begin and conclude August's nocturnal experience. August waits outside No. 44's door for the stranger to arrive; after appearing, he leads our narrator through that door and into the strange occurrences within his room and finally steps back "outside the door" with August, who finds himself transported back to the safety of his own room with the "door closed" (29–31). Doors, sometimes only partially opened, will continue to lead August through to 44 and even, at times, to nightmarish and out-of-body experiences (137, 145).

The idea of a door through which, or a threshold over which, one would travel to the subconscious regions of the self was a common enough belief even in Twain's day; however, in *Varieties,* James specifically invested this metaphor with theological implications. "If there be higher powers to impress us," he claims, "they may get access to us only through the subliminal door" (224). Thus James refuses to limit his concept of the subconscious solely to the "lower manifestations of the Subliminal," wherein a potpourri of "inattentively" gathered "sense-material" works in combination with the "subconsciously remembered" to determine conscious thought and action (223). Rather, the subliminal, as James speculates, may provide access to a power outside the influences of determining forces:

> But just as our primary wide-awake consciousness throws open our senses to the touch of things material, so it is logically conceivable that *if there be* higher spiritual agencies that can directly touch us, the psychological condition of their doing so *might be* our possession of a subconscious region which alone should yield access to them. The hubbub of the waking life might close a door which in the dreamy Subliminal might remain ajar or open. (223)

Although James's statement hardly proves the case for the existence of subconscious or spiritual experience, it does reveal, to some degree, his own concept of the divided self.

On the one hand, his "if" and "might" reveal both a resistance and a willingness to believe in a higher power, perhaps even a divine one; on the other hand, the channeling of that power through a theoretical subconscious humanizes the divine. This is precisely the point James finally reaches in the "Postscript" to *Varieties,* where he concludes that we "can experience union with *something* larger than ourselves" (James's italics), a "power" that may be a "larger and more godlike self" (468). Yet before following James into his notion of "conversion," which effectively unifies "sub" and "liminal" selves within that "something," we need to further consider Twain's fictional account of an encounter with what we might now hazard calling, borrowing James's term, a subliminal godlike self.

Much like the chaos James posited in the apparent upspring of subliminal thought, Twain's expressive narrative style, after the initial meeting between 44 and August, appears at first glance to be as directionless as 44's mental wanderings come to be. Plots open upon authorial whim while anecdotes collapse into the closureless space of the text, characters arrive and depart through tenuously associative vignettes, and the center, though barely holding, is elusive. No doubt it was this stylistic incongruity, much a part of Twain's later writings, which prevented many earlier critics from seriously accepting his fictional experiments with his dreamlike descriptions of subconscious activity, or what we might even call subliminal narratives. Aside from the critical resistance of Hill and Cox to Twain's work, Leslie Fiedler found Twain's tale of his mysterious stranger "crude and sophomoric," and even William Gibson, whose publication of the manuscripts in 1969 finally laid to rest the fraudulent claims of Paine and Duneka, suggests that further revision of Twain's texts by someone "more sympathetic to Twain's divided mind" may deliver a better text in the future.[43] We can only hope that no one attempts this task. Better to return to James in an attempt to read Twain on his own grounds—no matter what the complications.

To recast James's psychological profile of the divided self, both the plot of Twain's text and the figured mental meanderings of the mys-

---

43. See Gibson's introductory remarks to the *Mysterious Stranger Manuscripts,* 34.

terious stranger take on a resonant, yet heterogeneous personality of their own as they move through and within what James called a "series of zig-zags," with "one tendency" sparring with another, exhibiting the "wayward impulses" of a fictional experiment while struggling to "repair" artistic "misdemeanors and mistakes" (*Varieties,* 157). To borrow the explanation of the dreaming mind given by August Feldner in his description of 44's strange articulations, an outline that also defines Twain's stylistic maneuvers, the "dream-memory," which is scattered and "pretty capricious," often erupts in a "skipping and disconnected fashion," and "without apology or explanation" it "sidetrack[s] a subject right in the middle of a sentence if another" suits its fancy (158). Within both the self-imposed fictive boundaries of Twain and the theoretical parameters of James's work, then, 44 certainly appears as a prime example of a "heterogeneous personality."

Twain's subliminal path to another, or at least more extensive, god-like self is as searchingly complex and curious as James's, yet different. We have seen how James speculated on the existence of a secondary consciousness or even a superior part of the primary consciousness as early as his *Psychology.* However, in *Psychology,* he was far from convinced that these secondary characters really lay apart from the larger field of conscious experience. James's theory of "fringe" relations, ideas within our stream of thought of which "we are only aware in the penumbral nascent way," seems to account for the subliminal activity of other possible selves within a limit of personal contiguity (1:259). To the James of the *Psychology,* all our thoughts are constantly sensed within this fringe of "unarticulated affinities" often creating a "gap" in our understanding, and the bridging of this gap may bring with it the sense of encountering something outside the self (1:259–60). However, by the time of the writing of *Varieties,* James seems more willing to accept the existence of at least two independent or separately existing levels of consciousness or different psychic entities, one within the "subliminal region" of the mind and the other within the "level of full sunlit consciousness" (433). James's tentative thinking upon this duality of being reveals the state of development of psychological research at the time and is representative of the speculations of his fellow psychical researchers, which again brings us back to Twain and his own depiction and exploration of a divided mind in *No. 44.*

Twain makes the idea of inward division even more complicated than James does by dividing the self into three distinct entities. This aspect of its complexity begins with the introduction of duplicate characters into the life of the Rosenfeld Castle. Forty-four creates a set of duplicate workers in response to a printer's strike, which adds to the disruptive affect of fragmentation and also allows Twain to contemporize his tale's events; the whole question of economic and political authority is brought into play as the duplicates become scabs, taking the jobs of striking union workers. More important for my concerns, these duplicates enable Twain to develop fictionally his triadic theory of the self. Although August's own duplicate represents his dream self, he soon discovers from 44 that the mysterious stranger finally stands apart from both dream self and conscious self as yet another, third entity, what Twain, perhaps alarmingly, calls the "Soul" (124). This tripartition furthers the central action and an engagement of a spiritual or subliminal fringe of selfhood, one that our narrator soon discovers can be confining and threatening as well as liberating.

In a scene again representative of a dream, in which the stranger materializes in August's room summoning up the tastiest of foods and the best of tobaccos, spiriting from one subject to another, 44 explains the nature of the duplicates to a befuddled August:

> You know, of course, that you are not one person, but two. One is your Workaday-Self, and 'tends to business,' the other is your Dream-Self, and has no responsibilities, and cares only for romance and excursions and adventure. It sleeps when your other self is awake; when your other self sleeps, your Dream-Self has full control, and does as it pleases. It has far more imagination than has the Workaday-Self. Therefore its pains and pleasures are far more real and intense than are those of the other self, and its adventures correspondingly picturesque and extraordinary. (97)

Echoing a similar theory that he had first expressed in "My Platonic Sweetheart," Twain presents his duplicates here as incarnate imaginations, as a part of the self that imagines itself without conscious inhibitions. In psychological terms, Twain's duplicates, or dream selves, wander freely in a region that may well anticipate what we learned later about the subconscious.[44]

Twain's psychic division, moreover, points toward an even further separation of selves or personality split. Forty-four's "fleshing" of August's dream self, his duplicate, brings the narrator to the conclusion that our divided selves coexist like "Box and Cox lodgers" in a single "chamber," only encountering each other briefly over that "dim and hazy and sleepy half-moment on the threshold, when one [is] coming in and the other going out" (*No. 44*, 125). This dimness or haziness calls up James's idea of a suffusive fringe, though Twain incarnates the "coming" and "going" of vague imagistic figures with imagined flesh and declares their eminent superiority. Intellectually, emotionally, and imaginatively, August explains, I "was as a lightning bug to the lightning," as "phosphorus" to "fire" (126). And aside from his superiority, we soon discover that Schwarz, August's own duplicate, is entirely liberated from August's inhibitions, as this dream "sprite" wastes little time in successfully seducing Marget Regen, August's own sweetheart whose persistent purity had kept his own advances at a distance. Schwarz truly lives the life of which August only dreams. In this sense, we can say that he lives an alternate life or provides an alternate outlet for authorial and narratorial desire and freedom.

However, in Twain's tale the narrator cannot share in the freedom of his dream self; rather they exist as independent entities and, as the story progresses, they struggle with one another for the love of Marget. This struggle allows Twain to continue to develop his notion of the subliminal while complicating matters by introducing that third part of his divisional triad: the "Soul." August explains 44's message that, aside from the "Waking-Self" and "Dream-Self," each one of us contains a "Soul" that is released from the limitations of "encumbering flesh" and "able to exhibit forces, passions and emotions of a quite tremendously effective character" (124). August, whom 44 by now has given the power of vanishing at will, speculates that when invisible, "my soul" or "immortal spirit" is indeed freed from its limiting thoughts, a freedom that 44 has exercised throughout the story.

44. Though no record exists of his having read Dostoyevsky, Twain's spiritualized self notably shares certain characteristics with Dostoyevsky's phantasmal other in *The Double*. Yet unlike Dostoyevsky's presentation of the intermingling of selves, which ends in a psychological breakdown and leaves itself open to Freudian interpretation, Twain's opens into the possibility of a regenerative experience.

August's sense of unlimited freedom and the invisible flights of his soul allow Twain to approach the threshold of dreams from yet another angle, that of hypnotism. By "ferreting out of [his] memory certain scraps and shreds of information garnered from 44's talks," August determines that he can invisibly command his sweetheart's affections and actually capture the girl of his dreams. As August is quick to notice, his spiritual presence acted upon Marget "hypnotically," plunging her into a "somnambulic sleep" while releasing her "Dream-Self," free of inhibitions, into his arms (124). Both August and Schwarz then take turns frolicking with Marget on the sofa as their desires and wishes are satisfied in one of Twain's most sexually evocative scenes with "heaving breast, the deep sigh" and the "unrelaxing embrace" giving way to the "shouldered-pillowed head, the bliss-dimmed eyes" and the "lingering kiss" (128). However, unlike his dream self, and perhaps under the constraint of a Victorian conscience, August marries his mesmerized sweetheart.

Twain's representation of the dream self and the soul, as well as the hypnotically induced sonambulic condition, all figure his ongoing belief in alternate personalities. Twain, like James and other psychical researchers of the time, described these personalities as superior selves. Twain's mysterious stranger clearly reveals his superiority in terms of power over both the narrator and his dream self. However, 44 begins to diminish as his world claims more and more of August's time; inversely, August lays claim to the stranger's world, one that, to borrow James's words, is an "altogether other dimension of existence from the sensible and merely 'understandable' world" (*Varieties,* 460).

Conversion and Revelation

The stranger leads August into that inner clash of existential alternatives that James situated in the mind of the sick soul, such as a Tolstoy, Bunyan, or even a Twain. As narrator, August has already come to realize that the world he has helped to imagine forth is "frankly and hysterically insane," as 44 ultimately reveals in his concluding words; pain and cruelty are in a large part the result of humanity's inferior dreams. To return to the opening images, we might recall how August undercuts the paradisal atmosphere of Eseldorf with his descriptions of the villagers as numbly asleep. He describes the village priest, in particular, as "dissolute and profane and malicious," one whose "braying" is to be heard over and above that of the other asses in Eseldorf (5). Although August admires his master, he describes his master's wife and stepdaughter as little more than viciously scheming demons who, along with the castle's phony magician, are blinded by their own evil (13–14). The printers fare no better through August's narration; they are described as being either selfish, ignorant, and hopelessly alcoholic or as "malicious, hateful . . . underhanded and cruel" (15). Little wonder that August finds refuge in the fresh vision of 44.

August's conversion to 44's final and redeeming perspective, however, comes slowly. He is gradually led into a better way of dreaming or imagining the world through his continual relations with 44 or with that superior level of the self that 44 portrays. Two such encounters, in particular, lead August to create better fictions through the telling of his narrative, which is perhaps the only real proof of his conversion experience. Here Twain relies on well-known religious imagery for the effects of these pivotal encounters. In an image reminiscent of a eucharistic miracle that Twain includes earlier in his tale, one in which Jesus appears upon the host "in the form of a young man of wondrous beauty," 44 reveals to August a similar splendor in two important scenes.

The first occurs when 44 apparently allows Eseldorf's magician to destroy him. In astonishment, August explains how "a blot of black darkness fell upon the place and extinguished us all; the next moment in our midst stood that slender figure transformed to a core of dazzling white fire; in the succeeding moment it crumbled to ashes and we were blotted out in the black darkness again" (91). Later, in an equally important turn of the plot, 44 reaffirms his immortality as he materializes for a chosen few in a similar manner following a "great light" in his "white glory" and "unearthly splendor . . . supernal beauty and his gracious youth." For "it was from him," August explains, "that flooding light came, for all his form was clothed in that immortal fire, and flashing like the sun" (172–73). The scene itself closely parallels the apparition of St. Michael as Twain described it in his *Joan of Arc*. Joan, too, was "clothed in the awful splendor" radiating from her angelic visitor, and within that "immortal light," she too was "flooded" with its "transforming glory." In comparing Joan's experience of such a blinding light to "our dreams and imaginings,"

Twain connects both August and Joan within his dream theory.[45] More importantly, both of these scenes frame August's gradual acceptance of his own immortal spirit, the last being significantly characteristic of that transformative surge of religious conversion.

Both scenes also point to what Carl F. Keppler reveals as a literary figuring of the "second self as Saviour," as the "Christ-like in man, which is always the essential characteristic of the good second self."[46] Although Keppler ignores the doubling motif in Twain's fiction, he delineates the religious or spiritual dimensions essential to its shaping power in other psychic Bildungsromane like *No. 44*. Not that the second self is Christ, as Keppler explains, but rather it delivers over latent and efficacious impulses from unknown regions of the self. Turning to these regions, Twain unearths that "rarer" and "genuinely good" interior deliverer, perhaps no more than a "strange, expanded version of what one is," as Keppler speculates, or no less than a liberating agent for what one could be.[47] The important point for Twain and James is that the other side of self, rather than an essentially evil influence, as commonly portrayed in the literature of doubling, or the bearer of psychotic ills, as psychoanalysis generally defined it, is a potential conduit for spiritually enlightening experience.

In fact, James's chapter "Conversion" reveals that more than a few transformative experiences begin with sudden illumination. He begins that chapter with a lengthy quotation from a Mr. Bradley who claimed to have seen the "Savior, by faith, in human shape," momentarily appearing with "arms extended," inviting him unto himself. Later, he quotes another convert who described his experience as centered on the ineffable touch of "Christ with all his brightness and power" and followed by a glorious awareness of a complete personality change in which "all things" were created anew (*Varieties,* 175, 189). These testimonies, in particular, strikingly resemble the transformation of Twain's narrator, whose revelations, like a "single sudden flash" of "lightning," convey "infinitely sublime" thought (100–1). But the revelations are found within what Twain dubs as the "august empire of Dreams" (*No. 44,* 152), or rather that region of his narra-

45. Twain, *Joan of Arc,* 1:86–87.
46. C. F. Keppler, *The Literature of the Second Self,* 100. Keppler's book offers an original guide to literary doubling.
47. Ibid., 99–100.

tor's being that, normally closed to waking consciousness, erupts with all the power of religious truth.

However, they need not be beyond natural boundaries. That the saving grace may arise from within is the argument both Twain and James wish to make. "Psychology and religion are thus in perfect harmony up to [a] point," as James notes in the *Varieties*, "since both admit that there are forces seemingly outside of the conscious individual that bring redemption to his life," but such redemptive powers need not "transcend the individual's personality," James continues, nor must we insist that they are "direct supernatural operations of the Deity" (196). Like James, Twain refuses to identify transformative forces with the traditional concept of God. Twain's 44 rejects the "reverence" August attempts to offer him after the stranger's angelic illumination, and he even undermines the traditional Christian reading of his Christlike flashes of divinity, "effects" much better than those of "Barnum and Bailey," 44 explains, but still along the same lines. Perhaps Twain could accept the experiential effects, then, and perhaps he needed and longed for such a metamorphosis, but he only obliquely paid tribute to the beauty of the idea of such a transcendent experience. Although implicitly "transubstantiating," we might rather use the word "transmarginal" to describe August's relations with 44, a term James used to expand on the notion of subliminal thought (*Varieties*, 433).

Although similar to Myer's concept of the "subliminal self," James's notion of transmarginal experience incorporates his basic theory of the "stream of thought." Our thinking, according to James, consists of the "entire wave of consciousness or field of objects present to the thought at any time," and as "our mental fields succeed one another," certain objects recede toward faintly drawn margins of thought as our "centre of interest" shifts (*Varieties*, 214). The margin of the conscious field, then, though indeterminate in itself, allows some thinkers a larger field of play, continuously impinging upon thought while positioning, like a free-wheeling combination lock, optional objects of the same. Although we can consciously recall them or not, "our whole past store of memories *floats* beyond this margin, ready at a touch to come in," as James explains, "and the entire mass of residual powers, impulses, and knowledges that constitute our empirical self stretches continuously beyond it," allowing for a creative freedom outside the boundaries of determining margins (*Varieties*, 214–15).

Characteristically, James left his notion of the transmarginal self wide open for interpretation. By definition, he was not willing to prescribe or even stipulate the dimensions of the transmarginal, the reach of this latent stream of thought, nor would he define away the "beyond" of its stretch. In his final report on psychical research, "The Confidences of a 'Psychical Researcher,'" James hypothesized upon a "continuum of cosmic consciousness":

> Out of my experience, such as it is (and it is limited enough), one fixed conclusion dogmatically emerges, and that is this, that we with our lives are like islands in the sea, or like trees in the forest. The maple and the pine may whisper to each other with their leaves, and Conanicut and Newport hear each other's foghorns. But the trees also commingle their roots in the darkness underground, and the islands hang together through the ocean's bottom.[48]

Such speculation would expand the transmarginal into limitless space or even into a proto-Jungian image of consciousness. Although a later James was willing to believe that we might release our minds into a common experiential pool, "plunge" into a "mother-sea or reservoir" where "fitful influences from beyond leak in," in his *Varieties* he merely leaves the door open for the possibility.[49]

Twain, on the other hand, leaps unabashedly through that door in his own presentation of such Jamesian transmarginal streams. His 44 not only emerges as his narrator's transmarginal self, that wider stream of a potentially powerful synthesis of thought, but also as the ocean of thought from which all creation springs. Struggling to articulate this timeless, limitless, and measureless nature of generative thought, 44 despairs of "enlightening" the mind of his Augustan "other." "If it only had some capacity, some depth, or breadth," he explains, "but you see it does not hold anything" and, he continues,

48. "The Confidences of a 'Psychical Researcher'" was first published in *American Magazine,* October 1909. My text here is taken from *William James: Writings, 1902–1910,* 1263–64.

49. James met Jung only briefly while attending the Clark University conference in 1909. Though he had mixed reactions to Freud, James was impressed by Jung. Unlike Jung, however, James believed subconscious or unconscious regions of the mind provided access to a range of knowledge wider than that of a collective human unconscious.

"one cannot pour the starred and shoreless expanses of the universe into a jug" (114).

Twain's stranger continues his explanation of his exceptional mental capacities, and he echoes James's distinction between conscious and transmarginal fields of thought:

> [The] mind is merely a machine . . . it cannot conceive of a *new* thing . . . it can only gather material from the outside and combine it into new *forms* and patterns. . . . a man's mind cannot *create*—a god's can, and my race can. That is the difference. We need no contributed materials, we *create* them—out of thought. All things that exist were made out of thought—and out of nothing else. (115)

Twain crossed the conventional lines of psychology, philosophy, and religion by crafting a passage of discourse that passes beyond the normative literary boundaries of his time, and that acts as a brilliant and radical figure of 44's capacity to pass into the ontological mystery of things:

> And he remarked—the booming of the great castle clock mixing with his words—
>
> "again. eleven striking goes! she There word . . . my you give I least, the in not least; the in had, I've trouble the mind shan't I that, like picturesque, and showy something or pulverized, or burnt, him get and way, magnificent this in now, completed, it get I when and before; love of labor mere a in felt ever hardly have I as such satisfaction of sense a and it in pride . . . a feel I and thought, nor labor neither spared I've centuries; in out planned I've anything than it in interest more taken I've reputation; that with pains of lot a taken I've know You. . . . certainly. moral dead a to burnt, him get and lived, ever that magician glorious most the him make and Hoffman, Balthasar for building been I've reputation the perfect and out round will and Yes,"—
>
> My brain was spinning, it was audibly whizzing, I rose reeling, and was falling lifeless to the floor, when 44 caught me. His touch restored, and he said—
>
> "I see it is too much for you, you cannot endure it, you would go mad . . . Go and come as you please, amuse yourself as you choose." (179–80)

The passage follows and literally and systematically reverses an earlier passage that explains 44's devious plan to destroy the reputation of Balthasar Hoffman, the spurious magician whose false pretensions aggravate 44. By attributing the backward turning of time to the magician, 44 hopes to have him burnt at the hands of the superstitious peasantry.

Little wonder that August's head spins beneath the metaphysical weight, however. His world has just been turned around and thrust backward by 44, and the conversation he and 44 had shared only moments before has now returned back upon August as an overwhelming rush of image and sound. Linguistic signposts blur and cognitive boundaries rupture, and for the moment, August is left to fend for himself among the fragments of potential meaning.

Twain's reversal of the text, moreover, "undoes" the original and thereby reverses any idea that either reason or God's eternal word controls our fate. In earlier versions of Twain's tale, interestingly enough, 44 had been given the name of "Satan," and 44's seemingly irrational rush of words, his speech in reverse, echoes the satanic tradition of countering the Logos by presenting texts backwards. Such a rearrangement not only disrupts the unity and harmony of a logocentric universe but repositions responsibility for the making of order from chaos. The locus of creation now finds its place in the human mind and not necessarily, or solely, within the realm of rational relation.

Twain's reverse ordering of word and image, that is to say, leaves the reader temporarily lost in a chaotic influx of words and images. His synchronistic presentation of language taxes our usual diachronous sense of it, one conditioned to recognize a particular set of meaningful relations between words, phrases, and clauses. In effect, Twain releases textual constraints, and we are momentarily set free of the authority of grammatical antecedents, and thus of the history that informs them, as Twain invites us to participate in re-ordering a new set of significant relations. Much like his juggling of fact and fiction in the front matter of *Joan of Arc,* and more or less throughout the story, Twain's syntactical violations urge his readers to respond actively by creating some sense of order and meaning.

Twain's revelatory humor here points to the irony of our situation. Before we can engage our freedom to create or produce meaning, we need to constrain our thinking in some orderly fashion—or, rather, we express and experience our freedom through the process of fashioning significant constraints upon it. Two particular phrases from Twain's synchronistic passage, for example, call forth such a productive response. "Magnificent this in now" and "a feel I and thought" nearly satisfy the ear even while the eye struggles to rearrange nouns, verbs, and articles. Consciously selecting a new order allows for a rereading of the words "and I feel a thought in this magnificent now." Twain's passage as a whole thrusts us into the felt presence of word and thought and posits our thinking in the "now." Twain's text, in other words, provokes the independent thought that it fictionally posits as a reality, as it calls upon the reader to make a concerted effort to think apart from verbal and historical constraints.

However, along with *Huckleberry Finn,* both *Joan of Arc* and *No. 44* suggest that more than the known self emerges through such reflective effort. For instance, Twain presents Joan's attempts to understand the divine will as leading her into a cooperative participation in it, an empowering encounter with the other implicitly experienced in a dreamlike state. Huck's own experience within the Mississippi River fog alludes to a similar encounter, though we find him only reluctantly submitting to, then resisting, the potential revelatory power of the experience. His reflective struggle aboard the raft, however, leads him back into a similar liminal state of mind, as he thinks himself to the margins of his socially constructed identity.

Twain uses the image of fog in *No. 44* as well, having August's dream self, in his efforts to understand his conscious other, complain about the haze of thick thought in which he finds himself. As Huck might account for the befuddlement of August's dream self, "Nothing don't look natural nor sound natural in a fog"; the same might be said for August when he finds himself lost in an unnatural order of words. Both situations leave our narrators floundering for recognizable boundaries, though with his later hero, Twain feels more competent to depict the journey across and outside these boundaries. In allowing 44 synchronistically to present time and language in reverse order, Twain not only attempts to draw his readers into a more participatory role but also to figure forth that liminal experience that leads his heroes into their transformative encounters with the subliminal other.[50]

50. For an important cultural concept of liminality, see the work of Victor and

Like Huck, when released from the self's recognizable boundaries, August reels through a dizzying stream of strange sounds and images. His dream self speaks for August's own thoughts as it cries bewildered to our equally muddled narrator, "but it's fog, fog, fog . . . just a riddle" (150). The words of the dream self accurately reflect the thoughts of August, who also feels as if he is wandering through a fog of "unimaginable incomprehensibilities" (150). However, August's "extramarginal" other begins to ease his conscious brother by insisting that although he himself is a "spirit of the air," he is no less the "inhabitant of the august Empire of Dreams" (152). Twain's well-placed pun serves to prepare the reader for his reflexive conclusion and, at the same time, posits the three selves he theoretically constructs within one mind.

Here we seem to have arrived at a paradox, one that Twain leaves as it is. Much like the religious mystery of the "trinity," what we are left with is the possibility of contemplating three separate entities within one all-encompassing mind. Perhaps this is what James meant by a "Godlike" self, and even though he did not use this particular description in his *Psychology,* he prefigures its formulation in his theory of thought's stream. Within that stream other selves can be "thought in relation" and as in "one something," which is perhaps the only way we can verify the existence of anything at all (*Psychology,* 1:277). James's stream of thought thus allows for what he sees as a "Unity of Consciousness," a unity that is actualized and anchored, according to James, in one's "Thought" writ large (1:336, 338). Rather than merely denying the validity of subconscious "others," we can read 44's declaration that everything is "created" from "thought" as allowing for the inclusion of other selves from unknown regions of our entire stream of thought. August's initial bafflement, moreover, as he reacts to the revelations of 44 and his dreaming self or to the upthrust of thought from transmarginal regions, connects with a telling resonance to James's belief that this flooding of consciousness accounts for both religious experiences as well as to exceptional, if not original, visions of genius. Just as the primary field of consciousness maintains our link to the material word, James contends that if

---

Edith Turner, *Image and Pilgrimage in Christian Culture.* For the Turners, the liminal state of mind brings about a social disorientation from which it becomes possible for one to reformulate cultural identity.

"spiritual agencies" exist, the "psychological condition" of their touching us may be "our possession of a subconscious region which alone should yield access to them" (*Varieties,* 223). James and Twain, then, both posit the subconscious as a psychological entity, and both seem equally reluctant to close the doors upon its possibilities, possibilities that infinitely empower the range of human thinking.

In the penultimate chapter of *Varieties,* James underscores this idea of the expansive self, and in a final satiric jab at those who might find the terms *subliminal* or *transmarginal* "smelling too much of psychical research or other aberrations," James suggests calling that "abode" of "latent" power the "B-region" of our personality, or by any name one pleases, to distinguish it from the "A-region" of waking awareness:

> It contains . . . all our momentarily inactive memories, and it harbors the springs of all our obscurely motived passions, impulses, likes, dislikes, and prejudices. Our intuitions, hypotheses, fancies, superstitions, persuasions, convictions . . . all our non-rational operations, come from it. It is the source of our dreams . . . our life in hypnotic . . . conditions . . . our delusions, fixed ideas . . . [and] our supra-normal cognitions, if such there be. . . . (432)

Little wonder that Twain's fictional account of this Jamesian "B-region" carries us through abrupt shifts of plot and subject while the point of view slips through character and author and the psychological levels of each. We can empathize with Twain's narrator who, reeling beneath 44's revelation of this vast region, cries out that "it makes my brain whirl just to think of it" (114). But the pragmatic note that rings through both *No. 44* and *Varieties* declares the "whirl" to be worthwhile, even necessary, if the human mind is to continue enacting its thoughts upon the world. Twain declares as much and more in his tale's final chapter as he posits the mind, itself, as the only reality and its individual possessor as godlike creator.

In the final chapter of *No. 44,* Twain reverts to the presentational style of his earlier "What Is Man?" article. The dialogue recedes to a monologue as 44 departs, leaving us with his own gospel. His message, however, is as mixed as his tale. "Life itself is only a vision, a dream," he explains to August, one in which "nothing exists save empty space—and you," a you that is only a *"Thought*—a vagrant

Thought, a useless Thought, a homeless Thought, wandering forlorn among the empty eternities" (186–87).

Writing his final chapter in the year of the death of his wife Olivia, Twain was surely letting his sorrow seep into his stranger's parting words. In one register they are truly casting a nihilistic shadow back over the pages of his tale. However, at the same time they posit a godlike immortality, and Twain's "Thought," with its capital "T," reveals the author's belief, however flickering, in humanity's godlike creative powers. For it is our thought that allows us to dream, and it is our dreams that allow the emergence of "Thought," that "inextinguishable, indestructible" world "maker" (*No. 44,* 187). "Strange, indeed," 44 wonders aloud, "that you should not have suspected that your universe and its contents were only dreams, visions," and "fictions" (186). Then, 44 cites that particularly bad dream of a cruel and vengeful God as the most harmful thought of all, one that continues to fund an absurd image as worthy of belief: a God "who mouths mercy" and "Golden Rules and foreigeness [*sic*] multiplied by seventy times seven" and the promise of heaven for a chosen few, yet "invented hell" where the many will endure earthly "miseries and maladies of mind and body" for all eternity (186–87). Thus for Twain, heaven and hell and the world in-between have been built upon thought, thought that for the most part has worked to enslave the self within a limited vision.

New visions of reality can only be imagined by freeing the self in its entirety, that self that though undeniably determined in its actions is yet essentially free at its center. In the end, both Twain and James found freedom in the region of the self that ignites the future funding of knowable reality. To keep funding a reality that may be "so frankly and hysterically insane," as Twain's 44 stipulates, is to risk perpetuating a "grotesque and foolish dream," one that partakes of the evils it creates. But the "chance of salvation is enough" in itself to warrant the risk, James concludes, a chance whose possibility "makes the difference . . . between a life of which the keynote is resignation and the life of which the keynote is hope" (*Varieties,* 469). And in *No. 44, The Mysterious Stranger,* what we might call Twain's own fictive study of a variety of religious experience, he sounds a similar risky, pragmatic note from the concluding lines of his narrative of mind: "But I your poor servant have revealed you to yourself and set you free. Dream other dreams, and better. . . ." (186). With the self unveiled, Twain's closure leaps back and opens forward as a funding and final gift of human freedom.

Further Soundings

My own luck has been curious all my literary life; I never could tell a lie anybody would doubt, or a truth anyone would believe.

—Mark Twain, Notebook Entry, 1896

"*I* have always held the opinion," James wrote in an essay published just a month before his death, "that one of the first duties of a good reader is to summon other readers to the enjoyment of any unknown author of rare quality whom he may discover in his explorations."[1] In many ways, I have attempted to call attention to an "unknown author," or rather to a little-recognized side, or "rare quality," of an author we seem to know too well. I invite others to participate in the pleasure I have found in reading an unexpected—often surprising—side of Mark Twain.

Twain's more "serious" intent has certainly been noted by others before me, though more often than not it has been dismissed as a hindrance to his comic and literary performance. Although readers may no longer feel disappointed at not finding a joke within all of Twain's works, as Twain feared they would feel upon publication of *Joan of Arc,* they may still find his later fiction, with its often complex

---

1. William James, "A Pluralistic Mystic," in *William James: Writings, 1902–1910,* 1294. James wrote this brief essay in honor of Benjamin Paul Blood, a philosopher and James's friend. James claims that Blood's philosophy was quite similar to his own: "sometimes dialectic, sometimes poetic, and sometimes mystic in manner, sometimes monistic and sometimes pluralistic" (1295).

philosophical, psychological, and theological flights of fancy, uncomfortably alien.[2]

With Twain, familiarity has bred familiarity; along with the familiar has come the pleasure to be found in nurturing our expectations. However, such pleasure may soon dry up unless we risk moving beyond the parameters of the comfortably known. William James has made such an enabling move possible.

Limiting our study to the reading of a select few of Twain's works against James was a strategic choice. Twain, of course, was not merely a satellite of James, and though his portrayal of Huck, Joan, and August may be read as particularly responsive to James's line of thinking, other characters such as Hank Morgan and David Wilson remain less susceptible to Jamesian readings. In *A Connecticut Yankee in King Arthur's Court* and *Pudd'nhead Wilson,* neither Morgan nor Wilson experiences an encounter with the interior other that Twain depicts as essential to the liberty, if not the salvation, of Huck, Joan, and August. Twain does implicitly set his *Connecticut Yankee* within the framework of a dream; however, unlike his later dream narratives (especially *No. 44*) where he explores the relations between a waking and dreaming self, in Hank Morgan's dream of "Camelot," Twain focuses upon the reality of human ignorance and cruelty. The dream motif is used primarily as a method for transporting the reader into Twain's vision of Arthurian England and not as a means for describing the inner experience of creative freedom. In fact, both Morgan and Wilson argue more the case for a deterministic universe than for one determined by the thinking of independent minds. *Connecticut Yankee* and *Pudd'nhead Wilson,* however, allowed Twain to build fictionally upon his reading of Taine and Darwin, and both works reveal an ambivalence over the problem of human freedom markedly absent from the major works of William James.

In this respect, James seems to have been less convinced than Twain by the argument of "naturalism." Twain himself was drawn both toward and away from the tenets of naturalism as expressed by

---

2. Paine, *Mark Twain: A Biography,* 3:959. *Joan of Arc* "means more to me than anything I have ever undertaken," Paine recalls Twain saying, and his desire to refrain from attaching his pen name to it, at least in initial publication, affirms Twain's attempt to be taken seriously (959).

Zola, to whom Twain was ambivalently attracted. In discussing Zola's "fearful book, *La Terre*," Twain described it as a "ghastly nightmare," through which the reader is "whirled & buffeted helpless." Nevertheless, Zola seems to present a true picture of life, as Twain pointed out, and his characters "resemble the community" of people to be found in villages throughout America.[3]

Twain presents such a community in *Pudd'nhead Wilson*, a novel through which he directs his interest in the dual nature of the self toward the complexities of racial and social identity. Human will, fate, and choice are still the central issues in Twain's tale of displaced identities, one questioning the existence of racial difference itself. However, Twain presents all three as factors controlled by social context rather than by individual effort. Thus while Twain would continue to champion independent thought and its creative action in the world, ironically his faith in human freedom would never in itself be free of lingering doubt.

By no means, then, have I intended to suggest that the use of James completes our knowledge of Twain; James only provides another angle of vision and a different interpretive point of view. However, it is a point of view that has so far escaped any systematic investigation in the critical literature, and one, I would argue, that significantly expands our understanding of the later writings of Mark Twain. In brief, I have used James's work as an informing speculum to recuperate two late and very mistreated texts: Twain's *Personal Recollections of Joan of Arc* and *No. 44, The Mysterious Stranger*.

Reading Twain against James in a preliminary manner in Twain's *Adventures of Huckleberry Finn* allowed for a hypothetical revisioning of three of its often discussed scenes. Within these scenes, Twain was beginning to explore that "workshop of being, where we catch fact in the making," as James described it in his *Pragmatism,* "the actual turning-places and growing-places which they seem to be, of the world" (129). Within this existential workshop, Twain was only beginning to figure forth his theory of consciousness and his metaphysics of freedom; his more serious excursions into this central axis of being would find expression in his *Personal Recollections of Joan of Arc* and *No. 44, The Mysterious Stranger*.

Joan of Arc provided Twain with a subject through which he could

3. For Twain's comments on Zola, see Gribben, *Mark Twain's Library,* 2:797.

openly reflect upon the worth of religious experience within his metaphysical scheme, and a venue through which he could imaginatively redirect the facts to fund his liberating metaphysics. With de Conte as a first-person narrator, once removed from the intensity of Joan's own personal experience, Twain could move beyond the ineffable moments of religious experience, which had ultimately silenced Huck in a fog of unearthly voices, to an articulation of that experience in human terms. At the same time, de Conte's secondary first-person narration pointed to a particular frame of reference, one that in reflecting back upon its own interpretive limitations provokes a richer reading experience and suggests the possibility for Twain of freeing the self through its ultimate appropriation of the will of the divine other.[4]

Twain brought this encounter to even greater fruition in *No. 44*, as he struggled to create literary images that reflect a new vision of the human possibility for freedom in the face of an array of rather bleak reminders of the eternal presence of a cosmic determinism. As both narrator and the object of narration, August Feldner realizes his own freedom, both within the confines of language, as he attempts to describe the intrusive but liberating actions of 44, and outside its boundaries, as he ultimately releases narrative control and submits himself to the whims of his compelling other. In the end, these encounters are after all best and most usefully seen as a "variety of religious experience" fictionalized by Twain and theorized and speculated upon by William James.

Certainly a wider circle could be drawn in which to interpret Twain's religious, psychological, and philosophical reflections—in short, his metaphysics. Although not so vast as James's, his readings and friendships were as eclectic and diverse, while the often complex nature of his later works reveals his own desire to unravel ontological and epistemological mysteries. My goals here have been more modest and circumspect, however: to enrich our view of Mark Twain by situating his later works in a particular and perhaps unusual bel-

---

4. In *The Mind of the Novel,* Bruce Kawin points out that in experiencing what is ineffable, one is rarely capable of immediate articulation of the experience; words fail. A secondary first-person narrator provides a "something through which the nothing can be discussed" (146), as Kawin puts it, and for Twain, the "something" provides the necessary perspective through which to experience something more.

letristic context. Reading the later Mark Twain against William James provides a more comprehensive sense of Twain the man and artist, the thinker and writer, the teacher and humorist. The passion, irony, and occasional absurdity that come from the pages of his later works still evoke laughter—but a darker laughter, paradoxically of a more self-illuminating kind.

An Excursion on the Name/Number 44

*A*ugust Feldner's admission, in *No. 44,* that he was inferior to his dream self leads me to offer a brief excursus upon Twain's choice of his stranger's name: 44. "For he was my superior," August explains while relating himself to his interior other, and "my imagination, compared to his splendid dream-equipment, was as a lightning bug to the lightning." In another light, as August figures the distinctive difference, "I was phosphorous, he was fire" (126). While the dream self and 44 may or may not be one and the same in Twain's tale, they both surface as strangers from within August's mind; they both disclose, similarly, a superior side of Twain's narrator. Although no one has yet claimed James as an influence upon Twain's characterization here, I believe there is such a connection, and that it actually provides the most plausible explanation for Twain's choice of the name/number *44,* one that further links Twain and James in their efforts to describe the encounter of the self with the other.

As Sholom J. Kahn explains in *Mark Twain's Mysterious Stranger: A Study of the Manuscript Texts,* a book devoted to establishing the critical worth of the *Mysterious Stranger Manuscripts,* the name *44* has endured as one of Twain's tale's perplexing mysteries. Both erudite and readable, Kahn's book rehabilitates the *Stranger Manuscripts,* texts that have suffered from faulty and incomplete scholarship, as it provides a host of relevant detail leading up to and surrounding the production of Twain's texts. In discussing the use of the number *44,* a problem for which few details exist, Kahn suggests that perhaps Twain wanted "nothing more profound than a euphonious and alliterative number," which may be the case, though the number may point to an interest of Twain's particularly useful in understand-

155

ing his work.[1] Each of Kahn's explanations for Twain's using *44* offers at the very least another glimpse into Twain's ever-present comic sense and, at most, a useful lens for gaining a wider insight into a complex tale.

The speculations have been wide ranging. Henry Nash Smith suggests that Twain was expanding on a boyhood joke about Hannibal's Levin brothers. Indulging in childish wordplay, young Sam Clemens and his friends would delight in reminding the Levin brothers that "Twice Levin" is "Twenty-Two." Perhaps the older author still found some amusement in such playful antics: twice twenty-two, then, would be forty-four. Others have found more serious implications in Twain's choice of a number/name, pointing to the religious significance of *44* in terms of the doubling of the twenty-two letters in the Hebrew alphabet. Louis J. Budd suggests an even more direct influence through the work of the Polish dramatist, Adam Mackiewicz. While in Vienna in 1897, Twain dined with Theodore Leszetycki, his daughter Clara's piano teacher and one who would likely have known about Mackiewicz, a Polish martyr as well as revered artist. In his political discussions with Leszetycki, which were often lengthy, according to Clara, Twain may have heard about Mackiewicz's creation of a heroic savior for the Polish people in his *Forefather's Eve*: "forty-four."[2]

Other critics, however, such as William Gibson, express their desire to find a more general significance for the name/number, some suggesting it is a reflection of Twain's attitude toward the dehumanizing effect of ever-increasing social mechanization, and others pointing to the possibility of veiled religious meanings. Alternatively, the name may be little more than a practical joke, Twain playing illustratively on the doubling process denoted by his

---

1. Sholom J. Kahn, *Mark Twain's Mysterious Stranger: A Study of the Manuscript Texts*, 205–6. Kahn's study expands upon the work of Tuckey and Gibson and provides essential reading for any student of Twain and his *Mysterious Stranger Manuscripts*. I sympathize with Kahn's attempt to establish Twain as thinker; and I agree with him that Twain thought most about the problem of freedom, a problem he solves, to a large degree, in his figuring of selves in *No. 44, The Mysterious Stranger*.

2. Louis J. Budd, "Another Stab at the Origin of No. 44 as a Name," 1–3. Budd, himself, believes that in his introduction to *Mark Twain's Mysterious Stranger Manuscripts*, Gibson offers the most impressive evidence for Twain's use of *No. 44*.

own pseudonymous last name. The cipher may end in just that play, though Twain's own separation of identity along public and private lines becomes another problem of doubling that may still figure into his complex notion of self.

The number, then, may have a "multiplicity" of "interesting associations," as Kahn points out, though the worth of the varying speculations must rest upon whether Twain himself took the associations seriously.[3] Reducing his stranger's name to a cipher, in itself, suggests to me a certain seriousness in Twain's choice of names. He invites us to allegorize, to break the name's code. We are urged, in other words, to speculate upon hidden meanings. The stranger himself reveals one such meaning in the tale's conclusion, while pointing to the stripping function of reduction to cipher. He reveals himself to be a nonentity apart from August's dream imagination. Twain implies this same dreamy existence for his stranger by giving him the name of Philip Traum in his earlier "The Chronicle of Young Satan"—*Traum* being German for "dream." Indeed, 44 collapses dreams themselves into thought by his tale's conclusion, leaving us within the teleological framework of mind—a nonentity apart from our thinking.

Twain's interest in psychical research speaks for the amount of time and attention he invested in the study of mind. The foregoing chapters point to the general interest he took in the study of extraordinary mental states. Moreover, this book as a whole relates Twain's fictional theorizing upon such states to the work of William James. Even though no one has yet connected Twain's choice of *44* with his interest in James and psychical research, I believe he found the inspiration for his hero's name in James's *Psychology* and its discussion of what James called the "most famous case" of pathological doubling, that of Felida X (1:379–80).

It is worth quoting James at some length here, since the case of Felida X also casts some light upon Twain's own probing into psychical alterations and personality doubling, phenomena related in some sense, as Twain and James believed, to the effect of subliminal activity. James explained that Felida X began alternating personalities in early adolescence:

3. Kahn, *Mark Twain's Mysterious Stranger*, 206.

At the age of fourteen this woman began to pass into a "secondary" state characterized by a change in her general disposition and character, as if certain "inhibitions" previously existing, were suddenly removed. . . . At the age of *forty-four* the duration of the secondary state (which was on the whole superior in quality to the original state) had gained upon the latter so much as to occupy most of her time. (1:380, emphasis mine)

After offering a few more similar cases as evidence, examples to be found in both popular and academic publications, James offered a tentative yet important speculation insofar as it illuminates Twain's own psychical explorations.

In cases like Felida X's, he says, "in which the secondary character is superior to the first," the primary self appears the more inhibited of the two:

The word inhibition describes its dullness and melancholy. Felida X's original character was dull and melancholy in comparison with that which she later acquired, and the change may be regarded as the removal of inhibitions which had maintained themselves from earlier years. Such inhibitions we all know temporarily, when we can not recollect or in some other way command our mental resources. (1:381)

James's last few words are the most telling for both himself and Twain, both of whom placed the liberation of thought and action at a high premium within their work. Given Twain's reading of James's *Psychology* and his interest in multiple personalities, I suggest that Felida X's near-complete transformation into an apparently free and superior self at the age of forty-four provided Twain with a provocative example for his fictional case of an alternative self.

August's own transformation is made only gradually as he slips in and out of time and space with 44, shedding his inhibitions until he is ultimately careening about as capriciously as his mysterious guest. As a sixteen-year-old apprentice in master Stein's printshop, August has little power and even less authority until the manifestation of another stranger his age. Within the frame of Twain's narrative dream, it is tempting to interpret 44 as an embodiment of August's alter ego or even, in light of James's example of Felida X, as an eruption of an alternate personality. As happens with James's Felida X, there is a gradual shift from the "morbid" to the "superior," though the former is never entirely eradicated, as 44 slips in and out of August's thoughts; that is, August draws closer unto 44 until the two are indistinguishable.

As a unification of disparate selves, this gradual integration of 44 and August mirrors to some extent the experience of conversion James describes in his *Varieties*. In order to be converted one must be one of the "sick souls," as James puts it, who can never wholly live in the "light of good" while knowing "evil facts" to be a "genuine portion of reality" (152). This knowledge in itself divides sick-souled individuals, often leading to that dullness and melancholy preceding the emergence of a secondary personality. Conversion comes, in the psychological sense, when such individuals "find something welling up in the inner reaches of their consciousness, by which such extreme sadness could be overcome" (174). As James explains, this regenerative discovery can either come through an immediate illumination or over time through a gradual conditioning of one's mental or spiritual awareness. In either case, however, the experience leads to the tapping of a "new centre of personal energy" within the subliminal regions of the self (195). The sick soul becomes "twice-born," as James uses the term, finding "a stimulus, an excitement, a faith, a force that reinfuses the positive willingness to live, even in full presence of the evil perceptions that erewhile made life seem unbearable" (174–75). For August Feldner, that renewing stimulus to some degree arrives in his life as the mysterious stranger, No. 44.

Twain's 1884 Essay on "Mental Telepathy"

*T*aking the exceptional powers of mind seriously, especially in his later years, Twain offered his thoughts on the subject of telepathy in two separate articles: "Mental Telegraphy" and "Mental Telegraphy Again." *Harper's Magazine* published both articles, in 1891 and 1895 respectively, and they reveal that Twain's interest in the extraordinary play of mind was more than a passing fancy.

Twain had even provided a headnote to the 1891 essay explaining that he had been studying the seemingly telegraphic powers of mind for a number of years, "sixteen or seventeen" in all. His praise for the Society for Psychical Research and its work with telepathy bears repeating here. Twain's essay, moreover, suggests his continuing dialogue with the society as he refers throughout to their findings. Like its members, he seems to have been gathering substantial evidence of paranormal activity from books, newspapers, friends, and his own experience. In his own way, Twain considered his private probing into mysterious regions of thought to be part of the society's investigations:

> It is the same thing around the outer edges of which the Psychical Society of England began to grope (and play with) four or five years ago, and which they named "Telepathy." Within the last two or three years they have penetrated toward the heart of the matter, however, and have found out that the mind can act upon mind in a quite detailed and elaborate way over vast stretches of land and water. And they have succeeded in doing, by their credit and influence, what I could never have done—they have convinced the world that mental telepa-

thy is not a jest, but a fact . . . [and] have done our age a service—and a very great service, I think.[1]

Though the study of psychic phenomena would eventually claim its
share of prestige under the name of paranormal research, Twain may
have prematurely placed the world within the perspective of his own
convictions.

On a lighter note, we find Twain playing with his own notions of
paranormal activity in an article published in 1884 for the Society for
Psychical Research. To my knowledge, no one has ever published
Twain's article outside of the *Journal of Society for Psychical Research,*
and I offer it here as an example of Twain's early speculations on a
subject that would, along with its related interests, come to predom-
inate much of Twain's later work, especially his tale of the mysterious stranger.

Mark Twain on Thought-Transference

[The following characteristic letter from Mr. S. L. Clemens (Mark
Twain) will, doubtless, entertain many of our readers.—Ed.]

Hartford, Conn, October 4th, 1884.

Dear Sir,—I should be very glad indeed to be made a Member of
the Society for Psychical Research; for Thought-transference, as you
call it, or mental telegraphy as I have been in the habit of calling it,
has been a very strong interest with me for the past nine or ten years.
I have grown so accustomed to considering that all my powerful
impulses come to me from somebody else, that I often feel like a
mere amanuensis when I sit down to write a letter under the coer-
cion of a strong impulse: I consider that that other person is supply-
ing the thoughts to me, and that I am merely writing from dictation.
And I consider that when that other person does not supply me with
the thoughts, he has supplied me with the impulse, anyway: I never
seem to have any impulses of my own. Still, may be I get even by
unconsciously furnishing other people with impulses.

I have reaped an advantage from these years of constant observa-

---

1. Mark Twain, "Mental Telegraphy," 96.

tion. For instance, when I am suddenly and strongly moved to write a letter of inquiry, I generally don't write it—because I know that that other person is at that moment writing to tell me the thing I wanted to know,—I have moved him or he has moved me, I don't know which,—but anyway I don't need to write, and so I save labour. Of course I sometimes act upon my impulse without stopping to think. My cigars come to me from 1,200 miles away. A few days ago,— September 30th,—it suddenly, and very warmly occurred to me that an order made three weeks ago for cigars has as yet, for some unaccountable reason, received no attention. I immediately telegraphed to inquire what the matter was. At least I wrote the telegram and was about to send it down town, when the thought occurred to me, "This isn't necessary, they are doing something about the cigars now—this impulse has travelled to me 1,200 miles in half a second."

As I finished writing the above sentence a servant intruded here to say, "The cigars have arrived, and we haven't any money downstairs to pay the expressage." This is October 4th,—you see how serene my confidence was. The bill for the cigars arrived October 2nd, dated September 30th—I knew perfectly well they were doing something about the cigars that day, or I shouldn't have had that strong impulse to wire an inquiry.

So, by depending upon the trustworthiness of the mental telegraph, and refraining from using the electric one, I saved 50 cents— for the poor. [I am the poor.]

Companion instances to this have happened in my experience so frequently in the past nine years, that I could pour them out upon you to utter weariness. I have been saved the writing of many and many a letter by refusing to obey these strong impulses. I always knew the other fellow was sitting down to write when I got the impulse—so what could be the sense in both of us writing the same thing? People are always marvelling because their letters "cross" each other. If they would but squelch the impulse to write, there would not be any crossing, because the other fellow would write. I am politely making an exception, in your case; you have mentally telegraphed me to write, possibly, and I sit down at once and do it, without any shirking.

I began a chapter upon "Mental Telegraphy" in May, 1878, and added a paragraph to it now and then during two or three years; but I have never published it, because I judged that people would only laugh at it and think I was joking. I long ago decided to not publish it at all; but I have the old MS. by me yet, and I notice one thought in it which may be worth mentioning—to this effect: In my own case it has often been demonstrated that people can have crystal-clear mental communication with each other over vast distances. Doubtless to be able to do this the two minds have to be in a peculiarly favourable condition for the moment. Very well, then, why shouldn't some scientist find it possible to invent a way to create this condition of rapport between two minds, at will? Then we should drop the slow and cumbersome telephone and say, "Connect me with the brain of the chief of police at Peking." We shouldn't need to know the man's language; we should communicate by thought only, and say in a couple of minutes what couldn't be inflated into words in an hour and a-half. Telephones, telegraphs and words are too slow for this age; we must get something that is faster.—Truly yours,

S. L. Clemens.

P.S.—I do not mark this "private," there being nothing furtive about it or any misstatements in it. I wish you could have given me a call. It would have been a most welcome pleasure to me.

Two Letters from Twain to James

*M*y focus in this book has been on establishing an intellectual kinship between Twain and James, one built around their intricate involvement in similar ideas, desires, and purposes; however, the following letters provide a more intimate look into the friendship the two men shared. This friendship seems to have been built upon their first documented meeting in Florence, Italy, in 1892, where the men and their families were vacationing for reasons of health, hoping for both psychic and physical renewal. Twain's thoughts did indeed flourish as he began work on his *Joan of Arc,* and much of the time, his wife Livy found the climate particularly beneficial to her health. James, as well, was lifting himself from a mental paralysis of sorts during his stay in Florence, finding a new sense of pleasure in philosophical matters. The attempt to renew both mind and body would direct Twain and James along a common path as they examined everything from the benefits of mind cure and hypnotism to, as the following letters show, the therapeutic value of osteopathy and dietary supplements.

Twain first became interested in osteopathy, a medical treatment based upon muscular and skeletal manipulation, while in London in 1899. Intent upon finding relief, if not a cure, for his daughter Jean's epilepsy, Twain was intrigued by the news about Heinrick Kellgren and his osteopathic treatments. He committed himself and his family to the care of Kellgren during the summer of 1899, traveling to his sanatorium in Sanna, Sweden, to undergo what was then known as the "Swedish Movements Cure." Kellgren's treatment "appealed to both his imagination and his reason," as Paine records in Twain's biography, which was enough to arouse Twain's passionate commitment and inspire him to write to Joseph Twichell, one of his closest friends, that osteopathy must "prosper; it is common sense & scientific, & cures a wider range of ailments" than now cured by more traditional medical treatments.[1] For Twain, at least for a few years, osteopathy offered hope of overcoming the many physical sufferings he and his family would continue to endure.

At the same time, Plasmon, a food supplement developed by German pathologist Rudolf Virchow, captured Twain's attention. Twain would come to consider Plasmon as a complete food in itself, one that he would wholeheartedly endorse and promote in conjunction with the use of osteopathic manipulations. Not one to give an uniformed recommendation, Twain's own experience with this milk supplement reinforced his faith in its curative potential, as it had particularly aided in soothing his recurring bouts with indigestion. Twain's promotional motives, however, may have been tainted with his entrepreneurial designs. He had invested thousands of dollars in his belief in the therapeutic powers of Plasmon, purchasing stock in its British syndicate, and hoped to see it marketed worldwide. Twain would make little profit from his investment, however; more powerful investors would buy out his share in Plasmon's future.

As these letters to James reveal, he clearly believed in the regenerative powers of both osteopathy and Plasmon. At the same time, they reveal Twain's intimate knowledge of James's sufferings and a desire to ease if not end them. James had acquired an increasingly painful heart condition after an 1898 hiking expedition in the Adirondacks and, like the ailing Twain, sought to remedy his health problems. He too ventured outside the boundaries of ordinary medicine, bringing to bear on his illnesses an extraordinary array of potential treatments: hypnotism, mind cure, and various exercise and dietary regimens. Although James's letters to Twain—his "hearty words & splendid communications"—have not yet been discovered, we can imagine that his optimism for Kellgren was as high as Twain's own.

Along with the letters, I have included a transcription of a printed notice about Plasmon that Twain personally altered for James. It seems Twain was offering a friendly prescription of sorts, one guaranteed to please the palate.

1. Paine, *Mark Twain: A Biography,* 3: 1087–88.

30, Wellington Court,
Albert Gate.
London, Apl. 17, 1900.

Dear Professor James:

Mrs. Clemens & I have just returned from a few days' visit to Stanley at his country place, & find your letter awaiting attention.

I cannot tell you a tither of the pleasure your hearty words & splendid communications have given me, & I am very glad you did not put aside the impulse which prompted you to write them, but gave it hospitality. I am very glad indeed.

And I am also glad that you are moved to try Kellgren. That he can mend your disorder I do believe; that he will do you no sort of harm I am positive; I may even say I *know*. It is a strong word—I quite understand that. You are bound to get one advantage, happen what may: he will put your nerves & your circulation in better shape than they are now, & thus improve your general health.

The heart-cases which have come under my personal notice are three—my wife's, Clara Schumann's, & Frau von Kopf's.[2] He bettered Mrs. Clemens's case; he took hold of Miss S.'s case when she was no longer able to give lessons & earn her living; he presently enabled her to resume her work; hers is a bad case, but he keeps her going, & she doesn't die. But she cannot live without him. He has had her a year & a half, & has hopes of eventually curing her. Maybe he can; certainly no physician can. He has made her life quite tolerable—it was not that before.

Frau von Kopf is about 60. Thirteen years ago the Berlin specialists resigned her case & said she could not live more than two weeks. Ever since then Kellgren has treated her 2 months each year & secured for her 10 months of activity & comfort. For once (it was last year) she put off her arrival 2-months & went on a pleasure-journey, & came very near going under. With difficulty they conveyed her to Sweden from Hamburg—(K. practices in Sanna, Sweden, in Summer);

2. James's wife Alice had studied piano with Clara Schumann, who was an acquaintance of Twain's as well. No record, to my knowledge, exists documenting Frau von Kopf's relationship with either Twain or James.

& after a few days she was well again & climbing the hills with me, quite untroubled by her heart. She is a worshipper of Kellgren & will be very glad to pour some of it out on you when you give her a chance.

Stanley was on his deathbed with gastralgia in mid-February. I helped to put Lady Stanley on the track of Kellgren. He had Stanley back in the House of Commons in about a week. Yesterday Stanley said "Kellgren has been a godsend to me."[3] It is my conviction that Kellgren can modify *any* ailment, & can cure any that is curable. In typhoid, scarlet fever, influenza, & all such things, he is a master hand.

With cordial regards to you & yours from all of us,

Sincerely yours,

S. L. Clemens.

P.S. Ask me as many questions as you please: I shall be glad to answer.

30, Wellington Court,
Albert Gate.
April 23, 1900

Dear Professor James:

Indeed you are right in electing to go to Sweden instead of coming to England.

It is 4 1/2 hours by rail from the port—Gothenburg or Göteborg—to Jönkoping; then 3 miles by 2-horse landau to Sanna. Sanna con-

3. James seems to have known Sir Henry Stanley only through his reading of the famous explorer's African exploits; however, Twain's association with Stanley began in 1876, while both men were working as journalists. Twain would never become intimate friends with Stanley, however, though he would introduce him to Boston society during Stanley's first American lecture tour.

sists of half a dozen villas belonging to Kellgren—in these the patients live. It is on a vast blue lake, & at its back are the open fields. In the matter of brilliant skies, pure & bracing air, & intense quiet & repose-fulness, of course the place is perfection.

The rooms in the villas are small. Take no cat; you cannot swing her. However, one is out doors from breakfast till the daylight dies at midnight, the first half of the season, therefore one has no need of the rooms except for sleeping. The furniture is cheap but good enough, & there is no real overplus of it. I always felt so fresh & fine & young there, that I grew insanely fond of the place, & had to be bribed to leave it. And yet there are flies there—a [bird?] I never could endure.

The food is wholesome but exceedingly simple & free from vari-ety—it is *country* food & country style, & rationally prepared, noth-ing citified about it, & my family often mourned over it, but I got along plenty well enough with it.

If I were going there again I should do as I do now—live mainly on Plasmon (dissolved in *cold* milk) with Plasmon-cocoa for break-fast, fill-in with vegetables & fruit, & go without meat. This arrange-ment keeps a person well nourished, gives him a clear head & an unembarrased digestion, & saves him a lot of trouble & bother.

Plasmon is pure albumen & is extracted from skim-milk. I take 8 teaspoonfuls of the powder a day, in coffee, milk, chocolate, water, or anything that comes handy. Altogether it is 2 ounces, & is the equivalent of 2 pounds of fillet of beef, without the "stuffing" effect. However, I take it largely because it has kept me clear of indigestions for 2 months. I was weary of indigestions, as I had had one every night for 2 years. I have skipped plasmon only one day—& I had an indigestion that night. But I got up & cured it with a spoonful. I never dissolve it thoroughly, nor warm it; it is not necessary. I think it will digest any food it comes into contact with. I will send you Prof. Virchow's report.

Sincerely yours,

S. L. Clemens

PLASMON.
IMPORTANT NOTICE.

HOW TO DISSOLVE PLASMON:
Put the Plasmon into a cup ~~or saucepan~~. To every teaspoonful of the powder, add 2 tablespoonfuls of ~~tepid water or~~[4] milk; rub, with a spoon, into a jelly or paste; then add, ~~for every teaspoonful of Plasmon Powder, half a teacup of warm water or~~ milk; ~~place on the fire and bring to the boil~~. It is essential that stirring should be kept up the whole time.

If required as a soup, salt or any other flavouring might be added, if preferred.

4. Here, and also after the next stricken phrase, Twain inserted the word, "cold," indicating his strong preference for preparing Plasmon with cold milk.

Andrews, Kenneth R. *Nook Farm: Mark Twain's Hartford Circle*. Cambridge: Harvard University Press, 1950.

Barzun, Jacques. *A Stroll with William James*. New York: Harper and Row, 1983.

Bellamy, Gladys Carmen. *Mark Twain as a Literary Artist*. Norman: University of Oklahoma Press, 1950.

Binet, Alfred. *On Double Consciousness*. Chicago: Open Court Publishing Co., 1896.

Bjork, Daniel. *William James: The Center of His Vision*. New York: Columbia University Press, 1988.

Blair, Walter. *Mark Twain and Huckleberry Finn*. Berkeley: University of California Press, 1960.

Brashear, Minnie M. *Mark Twain: Son of Missouri*. 1934. New York: Russell and Russell, 1964.

Brennan, Bernard P. *The Ethics of William James*. New York: Bookman Associates, 1961.

Brodwin, Stanley. "Mark Twain's Masks of Satan: The Final Phase." *American Literature* 45 (1973): 202–27.

———. "Mark Twain's Theology: The Gods of a Brevet Presbyterian." In *The Cambridge Companion to Mark Twain,* ed. Forest G. Robinson. Cambridge: Cambridge University Press, 1995.

Brooks, Van Wyck. *The Ordeal of Mark Twain*. New York: E. P. Dutton, 1920.

Brown, Frank Burch. *Religious Aesthetics: A Theological Study of Making and Meaning*. Princeton: Princeton University Press, 1989.

Bruner, Jerome. *Actual Minds, Possible Worlds*. Cambridge: Harvard

University Press, 1986.

Budd, Louis J. "Another Stab at the Origin of No. 44 as a Name." *Mark Twain Circular* 3 (July–August 1989): 1–3.

———. *Our Mark Twain: The Making of His Public Personality.* Philadelphia: University of Pennsylvania Press, 1983.

Burgt, Robert J. *The Religious Philosophy of William James.* Chicago: Nelson-Hall, 1981.

Camfield, Gregg. *Sentimental Twain: Samuel Clemens in the Maze of Moral Philosophy.* Philadelphia: University of Pennsylvania Press, 1994.

Campbell, James. *The Community Reconstructs: The Meaning of Pragmatic Social Thought.* Urbana: University of Illinois Press, 1992.

Cavell, Stanley. *In Quest of the Ordinary: Lines of Skepticism and Romanticism.* Chicago: University of Chicago Press, 1988.

Clebsch, William A. *American Religious Thought: A History.* Chicago: University of Chicago Press, 1973.

Conkin, Paul K. *Puritans and Pragmatists: Eight Eminent American Thinkers.* New York: Putnam's, 1968.

Conn, Peter. *The Divided Mind.* New York: Cambridge University Press, 1983.

Cotkin, George. *William James: Public Philosopher.* Baltimore: Johns Hopkins University Press, 1990.

Cox, James M. *Mark Twain: The Fate of Humor.* Princeton: Princeton University Press, 1966.

Cummings, Sherwood. *Mark Twain and Science: Adventures of a Mind.* Baton Rouge: Louisiana State University Press, 1988.

Dewey, John. *Art as Experience.* New York: Putnam's, 1934.

Dolmetsch, Carl. *Our Famous Guest: Mark Twain in Vienna.* Athens: University of Georgia Press, 1992.

Dooley, Patrick K. *Pragmatism as Humanism: The Philosophy of William James.* Totawa, N.J.: Littlefield, 1975.

Dostoyevsky, F. M. *The Double: A Poem of St. Petersburg.* Trans. George Bird. Bloomington: Indiana University Press, 1958.

Doyno, Victor. *Writing "Huck Finn": Mark Twain's Creative Process.* Philadelphia: University of Pennsylvania Press, 1991.

Emerson, Ralph Waldo. "Nature." In *Ralph Waldo Emerson,* ed. Richard Poirier. Oxford: Oxford University Press, 1990.

Fabre, Lucien. *Joan of Arc.* Trans. Gerald Hopkins. London:

Odhams Press Limited, 1954.

Freud, Sigmund. *General Psychological Theory Papers on Metapsychology*. Ed. Philip Rieff. New York: Collier, 1963.

———. *The Interpretation of Dreams*. Trans. A. A. Brill. New York: Random, 1950. First published in 1900 as *Die Traumdeutung*.

Fuller, Robert C. *Americans and the Unconscious*. New York: Oxford University Press, 1986.

Gavin, William Joseph. *William James and the Reinstatement of the Vague*. Philadelphia: Temple University Press, 1992.

Gibson, William M. *The Art of Mark Twain*. New York: Oxford University Press, 1976.

Gies, Frances. *Joan of Arc: The Legend and the Reality*. New York: Harper and Row, 1959.

Gillman, Susan. *Dark Twins: Imposture and Identity in Mark Twain's America*. Chicago: University of Chicago Press, 1982.

Goodman, Nelson. *Of Minds and Other Matters*. Cambridge: Harvard University Press, 1984.

Gribben, Alan. *Mark Twain's Library: A Reconstruction*. 2 vols. Boston: G. K. Hall, 1980.

———. "When Other Amusements Fail: Mark Twain and the Occult." In *The Haunted Dusk: American Supernatural Fiction, 1820–1920*, ed. Howard Kerr. Athens: University of Georgia Press, 1983.

Gunn, Giles. *The Culture of Criticism and the Criticism of Culture*. New York: Oxford University Press, 1987.

———. *The Interpretation of Otherness: Literature, Religion, and the American Imagination*. New York: Oxford University Press, 1985.

———. *Thinking Across the American Grain: Ideology, Intellect, and the New Pragmatism*. Chicago: University of Chicago Press, 1992.

Gurney, Edmund, Frederick Myers, and Frank Podmore. *Phantasms of the Living*. 2 vols. London: Trubner, 1886.

Hale, Nathan. *Freud and the Americans: The Beginning of Psychoanalysis in the United States, 1876–1917*. New York: Oxford University Press, 1971.

Harnsberger, Caroline Thomas. *Mark Twain's Views of Religion*. Evanston, Ill.: Shori Press, 1961.

Harris, Susan K. *Mark Twain's Escape from Time: A Study in*

Patterns and Images. Columbia: University of Missouri Press, 1982.

Hassan, Ihab. *Selves at Risk: Patterns of Quest in Contemporary American Letters*. Madison: University of Wisconsin Press, 1990.

Hawthorne, Nathaniel. *The Blithedale Romance and Fanshawe*. 1852. In *The Centenary Edition of the Works of Nathaniel Hawthorne,* ed. William Charvat et al. Columbus: Ohio State University Press, 1964.

Hill, Hamlin. *Mark Twain: God's Fool*. New York: Harper and Row, 1973.

Hook, Sidney. *The Metaphysics of Pragmatism*. Chicago: Open Court Publishing Co., 1927.

Howells, William Dean. *My Mark Twain: Reminiscences and Criticisms*. New York: Harper and Row, 1910.

James, William. "The Dilemma of Determinism." In *The Will to Believe, and Other Essays in Popular Philosophy*. 1897. New York: Dover, 1956.

———. *Essays, Comments, and Reviews*. Cambridge: Harvard University Press, 1987.

———. *Essays in Psychical Research,* vol. 16 of *The Works of William James,* Cambridge: Harvard University Press, 1986.

———. "The Hidden Self." *Scribner's Magazine* 7 (1890): 361–73.

———. *Human Immortality: Two Supposed Objections to the Doctrine*. Boston: Houghton, 1898.

———. *The Letters of William James*. Ed. Henry James. 2 vols. Boston: Atlantic Monthly Press, 1920.

———. *The Meaning of Truth*. Ed. Fredson Bowers and Ignas Skrupskelis. Cambridge: Harvard University Press, 1975 [1909].

———. "On Some Omissions in Introspective Psychology." In *William James: Writings, 1878–1899,* ed. Gerald E. Myers. New York: Library of America, 1992.

———. *Pragmatism: A New Name for Some Old Ways of Thinking*. 1907. Ed. Bruce Kuklick. Indianapolis: Hackett Publishing Company, 1981.

———. *The Principles of Psychology*. 2 vols. 1890. New York: Henry Holt and Company, 1899.

———. *Psychology: The Briefer Course*. 1892. Ed. Gordon Allport. New York: Harper and Row, 1961.

———. Review of Breuer and Freud, "Verber den Psychischen

Mechanimos Hysterischer Phänomene," *Psychological Review,* 1 (March 1894): 199.

———. Review of Pierre Janet, "L'état Mental des Hystériques," *Psychological Review,* 1 (March 1894): 195–99.

———. *The Varieties of Religious Experience: A Study in Human Nature.* 1902. Ed. Bruce Kuklick. New York: Vintage, 1990.

———. "What Psychical Research Has Accomplished." In *William James on Psychical Research,* ed. Gardner Murphy and Robert C. Ballou. New York: Viking, 1960.

———. *William James: Writings 1902–1910.* Ed. Bruce Kuklick. New York: Library of America, 1987.

Jauss, H. R. "The Alterity and Modernity of Medieval Literature." *New Literary History* 10 (1979): 181–229.

———. "Horizon, Structure and Dialogicity." In *Question and Answer: Forms of Dialogic Understanding.* Minneapolis: University of Minnesota Press, 1989.

Jewkes, Wilfred T. *Joan of Arc: Fact, Legend, and Literature.* New York: Harcourt, 1964.

Johnson, Ellwood. "William James and the Art of Fiction." *Journal of Aesthetics and Art Criticism* 30 (1972): 285–96.

Johnson, James L. *Mark Twain and the Limits of Power: Emerson's God in Ruins.* Knoxville: University of Tennessee Press, 1982.

Kahn, Sholom J. *Mark Twain's Mysterious Stranger: A Study of the Manuscript Texts.* Columbia: University of Missouri Press, 1978.

Kaplan, Justin. *Mark Twain and His World.* London: Michael Joseph, 1974.

———. *Mr. Clemens and Mark Twain.* New York: Simon and Schuster, 1968.

Kawin, Bruce. *The Mind of the Novel: Reflexive Fiction and the Ineffable.* Princeton: Princeton University Press, 1982.

Keppler, C. F. *The Literature of the Second Self.* Tucson: University of Arizona Press, 1972.

Kerr, Howard. *Mediums, and Spirit-Rappers, and Roaring Radicals: Spiritualism in American Literature, 1850–1900.* Urbana: University of Illinois Press, 1972.

———, ed. *The Haunted Dusk: American Supernatural Fiction, 1820–1920.* Athens: University of Georgia Press, 1983.

King, John Owen. *The Iron of Melancholy: Structures of Spiritual Conversion in America from the Puritan Conscience to*

Victorian Neurosis. Middleton, Conn.: Wesleyan University Press, 1983.

Kuklick, Bruce. *The Rise of American Philosophy*. New Haven: Yale University Press, 1977.

Laing, R. D. *The Divided Self*. New York: Pantheon Books, 1960.

———. *Self and Others*. New York: Pantheon, 1969.

Lang, Andrew. *The Maid of France: Being the History of the Life and Death of Jeanne d'Arc*. New York: Longmans, 1909.

Lauber, John. *The Inventions of Mark Twain*. New York: Farrar, Straus and Giroux, 1990.

Lears, T. J. *No Place of Grace: Antimodernism and the Transformation of American Culture, 1880–1920*. New York: Pantheon, 1981.

Levinson, Henry Samuel. *The Religious Investigations of William James*. Chapel Hill: University of North Carolina Press, 1981.

Lewis, R. W. B. *The Jameses: A Family Narrative*. New York: Farrar, Straus and Giroux, 1991.

Lynch, Kathryn L. *The High Medieval Dream Vision: Poetry, Philosophy, and Literary Form*. Stanford: Stanford University Press, 1988.

Macnaughton, William R. *Mark Twain's Last Years as a Writer*. Columbia: University of Missouri Press, 1979.

Marr, David. *American Worlds Since Emerson*. Amherst: University of Massachusetts Press, 1988.

Matthiessen, F. O. *The James Family*. New York: Knopf, 1961.

Melville, Herman. *Moby-Dick*. 1851. New York: Norton, 1967.

Michelet, Jules. *Joan of Arc*. Trans. Albert Guerard. Ann Arbor: University of Michigan Press, 1957.

Michelson, Bruce. *Mark Twain on the Loose: A Comic Writer and the American Self*. Amherst: University of Massachusetts Press, 1995.

Münsterberg, Hugo. *Psychology and Life*. Boston: Houghton, 1899.

——— et al. *Subconscious Phenomena*. Boston: Gorham Press, 1910.

Myers, F. W. H. *Human Personality and Its Survival of Bodily Death*. New York: Longmans, 1904.

———. Review of *The Principles of Psychology*, by William James. In *Proceedings of the Society for Psychical Research*, 111–33. London: Kegan Paul, 1891–1892.

———. "The Subliminal Consciousness." In *Proceedings of the Society for Psychical Research*, 298–355. London: Kegan Paul, 1892.

Myers, Gerald. *William James: His Life and Thought*. New Haven: Yale University Press, 1986.

Nolan, Edward P. *Now Through a Glass Darkly: Specular Images of Being and Knowing from Virgil to Chaucer*. Ann Arbor: University of Michigan Press, 1990.

O'Connor, Leo F. *Religion in the American Novel: The Search for Belief, 1860–1920*. New York: University Press of America, 1984.

Paine, Albert Bigelow. *Mark Twain: A Biography*. 4 vols. New York: Harper and Brothers Publishers, 1912.

Pells, Richard. *Radical Visions and American Dreams*. New York: Harper and Row, 1973.

Perry, Lewis. *Intellectual Life in America: A History*. Chicago: University of Chicago Press, 1984.

Perry, Ralph Barton. *The Thought and Character of William James*. 2 vols. Boston: Little, Brown and Co., 1935.

Poe, Edgar Allan. *The Narrative of Arthur Gordon Pym*. 1838. In *Edgar Allan Poe: Poetry and Tales,* ed. Patrick F. Quinn. New York: Library of America, 1984.

———. "William Wilson." In *Edgar Allan Poe: Poetry and Tales,* ed. Patrick F. Quinn. New York: Library of America, 1984.

Poirier, Richard. *The Performing Self: Compositions and Decompositions in Languages of Contemporary Life*. New Brunswick: Rutgers University Press, 1992.

———. *Poetry and Pragmatism*. Cambridge: Harvard University Press, 1992.

———. *A World Elsewhere: The Place of Style in American Literature*. Madison: University of Wisconsin Press, 1985.

Posnock, Ross. *The Trial of Curiosity: Henry James, William James, and the Challenge of Modernity*. New York: Oxford University Press, 1991.

Priest, Stephen. *Theories of the Mind*. Boston: Houghton Mifflin, 1991.

Rae, Patricia. "William James in Contemporary Criticism." *Southern Review* 21 (1988): 307–14.

Raknem, Ingvald. *Joan of Arc in History, Legend and Literature*.

Oslo: Scandinavian University Books, 1971.

Ramsey, Bennett. *Submitting to Freedom: The Religious Vision of William James*. Oxford: Oxford University Press, 1993.

Regan, Robert. *Unpromising Heroes: Mark Twain and His Characters*. Berkeley: University of California Press, 1966.

Reynolds, David S. *Faith in Fiction: The Emergence of Religious Literature in America*. Cambridge: Harvard University Press, 1981.

Rogers, Robert. *A Psychoanalytic Study of the Double in American Literature*. Detroit: Wayne State University Press, 1970.

Rorty, Richard. *Consequences of Pragmatism*. Minneapolis: University of Minnesota Press, 1982.

———. *Contingency, Irony, and Solidarity*. Cambridge: Cambridge University Press, 1989.

———. *Philosophy and the Mirror of Nature*. Princeton: Princeton University Press, 1979.

Rosenblum, Nancy. *Another Liberalism: Romanticism and the Reconstruction of Liberal Thought*. Cambridge: Harvard University Press, 1987.

Royce, Josiah. *William James and Other Essays on the Philosophy of Life*. New York: The Macmillan Co., 1912.

Ruf, Frederick. *The Creation of Chaos: William James and the Stylistic Making of a Disorderly World*. Albany: State University of New York Press, 1991.

Salomon, Roger B. "Escape from History: Mark Twain's *Joan of Arc*." *Philological Quarterly* 40 (1961): 77–90.

Salvaggio, Ruth. "Twain's Later Phase Reconsidered: Duality and the Mind." *American Literature* 12 (1979): 322–29.

Santayana, George. *Character and Opinion in the United States*. New York: Scribner's, 1936.

———. *Interpretations of Poetry and Religion*. New York: Harper and Row, 1957.

Schwartz, Thomas D. "Mark Twain and Robert Ingersoll: The Free-thought Connection." *American Literature* 48 (1976): 182–93.

Searle, William. *The Saint and the Skeptics: Joan of Arc in the Work of Mark Twain, Anatole France, and Bernard Shaw*. Detroit: Wayne State University Press, 1976.

Shaw, George Bernard. *Saint Joan: A Chronicle Play in Six Scenes and an Epilogue*. Baltimore: Penguin, 1951.

Sidis, Boris, and Simon Goodhart. *Multiple Personality: An Experimental Investigation into the Nature of Human Individuality.* New York: D. Appleton and Co., 1904.

Smart, Ninian. *The Philosophy of Religion.* London: Oxford University Press, 1979.

Smith, Henry Nash. *Mark Twain: The Development of a Writer.* Cambridge: Harvard University Press, 1962.

Stahl, J. D. *Mark Twain, Culture and Gender: Envisioning America through Europe.* Athens: University of Georgia Press, 1994.

Stone, Albert E. *The Innocent Eye: Childhood in Mark Twain's Imagination.* New Haven: Yale University Press, 1961.

Strout, Cushing. *Making American Tradition: Visions and Revisions from Ben Franklin to Alice Walker.* New Brunswick, N.J.: Rutgers University Press, 1990.

Suckiel, Ellen K. *The Pragmatic Philosophy of William James.* South Bend: University of Notre Dame Press, 1982.

Taylor, Eugene. *William James on Exceptional Mental States: The 1896 Lowell Lectures.* Amherst: University of Massachusetts Press, 1984.

Thayer, H. S. *Meaning and Action: A Study of American Pragmatism.* Indianapolis: Bobbs-Merrill, 1973.

Tompkins, Jane. *Sensational Designs: The Cultural Work of American Fiction, 1790–1860.* New York: Oxford University Press, 1985.

Tuckey, John S. *Mark Twain and Little Satan.* West Lafayette, Ind.: Purdue University Studies, 1963.

Turner, Victor, and Edith Turner. *Image and Pilgrimage in Christian Culture.* New York: Oxford University Press, 1978.

Twain, Mark. *Adventures of Huckleberry Finn.* 1884. The Mark Twain Library. Ed. Walter Blair and Victor Fischer. Berkeley: University of California Press, 1985.

———. "As Regards Patriotism." In *A Pen Warmed-Up in Hell: Mark Twain in Protest,* ed. Frederick Anderson. New York: Harper and Row, 1972.

———. *The Autobiography of Mark Twain.* Ed. Charles Neider. New York: Harper and Row, 1959.

———. *Christian Science.* In *Uniform Edition of Mark Twain's Works.* New York: Harper and Row, 1907.

———. "The Chronicle of Young Satan." In *Mark Twain's*

Mysterious Stranger Manuscripts, ed. William M. Gibson. Berkeley: University of California Press, 1969.

———. *A Connecticut Yankee in King Arthur's Court.* 1889. Ed. Bernard L. Stein. The Mark Twain Library. Berkeley: University of California Press, 1979.

———. *The Devil's Race-Track: Mark Twain's Great Dark Writings.* Ed. John S. Tuckey. Berkeley: University of California Press, 1966.

———. "The Facts Concerning the Recent Carnival of Crime in Connecticut." In *Mark Twain's Collected Tales, Sketches, Speeches, and Essays,* 1891–1910, ed. Louis J. Budd. New York: Library of America, 1992.

———. *Mark Twain in Eruption: Hitherto Unpublished Pages about Men and Events.* Ed. Bernard DeVoto. New York: Harper and Row, 1940.

———. *Mark Twain's Letters.* Ed. Albert Bigelow Paine. 2 vols. New York: Harper and Row, 1917.

———. *Mark Twain: Letters from the Earth.* Ed. Bernard DeVoto. New York: Harper and Row, 1938.

———. "Mark Twain on Thought-Transference." *Journal of the Society for Psychical Research* 1 (1884–1885): 166–67.

———. *Mark Twain's Mysterious Stranger Manuscripts.* Ed. William M. Gibson. Berkeley: University of California Press, 1969.

———. *Mark Twain's Notebook.* Ed. Albert Bigelow Paine. New York: Harper and Row, 1935.

———. *Mark Twain's Own Autobiography: The Chapters from the North American Review.* Ed. Michael J. Kiskis. Madison: University of Wisconsin Press, 1990.

———. "Mental Telegraphy." In *The Science Fiction of Mark Twain,* ed. David Ketterer. Hamden, Conn.: Archon Books, 1984.

———. "My Platonic Sweetheart." Papers. Mark Twain Project, Bancroft Library, Berkeley.

———. *No. 44, The Mysterious Stranger.* The Mark Twain Library. Ed. John S. Tuckey. Text established by William M. Gibson and the Mark Twain Project. Berkeley: University of California Press, 1982. First published in 1969 in Gibson's *Mark Twain's Mysterious Stranger Manuscripts.*

———. *Personal Recollections of Joan of Arc.* 2 vols. 1896. New

York: Harper and Row, 1906.

———. "Saint Joan of Arc." In *The 30,000 Bequest and Other Stories*. Vol. 24 of *The Writings of Mark Twain*. Author's National Edition. New York: Harper and Row, 1906.

———. "Schoolhouse Hill." In *Mark Twain's Mysterious Stranger Manuscripts,* ed. William M. Gibson. Berkeley: University of California Press, 1969.

———. "The Secret History of Eddypus, the World Empire." In *Mark Twain's Fables of Man,* ed. John S. Tuckey. Berkeley: University of California Press, 1972.

———. *Selected Mark Twain–Howells Letters, 1872–1910*. Ed. Frederick Anderson et al. Cambridge: Harvard University Press, 1967.

———. "What Is Man?" In *What Is Man?, and Other Philosophical Writings,* ed. Paul Baender. Berkeley: University of California Press, 1973.

Wagenknecht, Edward. *Mark Twain: The Man and His Work*. New Haven: Yale University Press, 1935.

Weatherford, Roy. *The Implications of Determinism*. London: Routledge, 1991.

Welland, Dennis. *Mark Twain in England*. London: Chatto and Windus, 1978.

West, Cornell. *The American Evasion of Philosophy: A Genealogy of Pragmatism*. Madison: University of Wisconsin Press, 1989.

Yeazell, Ruth. *The Death and Letters of Alice James*. Berkeley: University of California Press, 1981.

Zwarg, Christina. "Woman as Force in Twain's *Joan of Arc*: The Unwordable Fascination." *Criticism* 27 (1985): 57–72.